Joanne Anderson has worked as a journalist on major newspapers in Australia and Hong Kong. She joined *The Age* in 2004, eventually becoming chief desk editor, a role in which she works with a team editing articles for online and print publication. She has overseen in-house style guides and written a weekly newsletter on English usage for staff at *The Age*, *The Sydney Morning Herald* and their sister outlets. Although a Melbourne resident, she does not like Aussie Rules.

* * *

Matt Golding is a Melbourne-based cartoonist whose work has appeared in *The Age* and *The Sydney Morning Herald* for two decades. Matt has a history of managing to write wrongly, even though his tiny pocket cartoons generally contain very few words. Jo has long been called upon to right his wrongs, and the making of this book was no exception. He too does not follow footy.

WRITELY

or

WRONGLY

An unstuffy guide to language stuff

JOANNE ANDERSON

WITH ILLUSTRATIONS BY
MATT GOLDING

murdoch books

Sydney | London

Published in 2023 by Murdoch Books, an imprint of Allen & Unwin
Text © Joanne Anderson 2023
Internal illustrations © Matt Golding 2023

Murdoch Books Australia
Cammeraygal Country
83 Alexander Street, Crows Nest NSW 2065
Phone: +61 (0)2 8425 0100
murdochbooks.com.au
info@murdochbooks.com.au

Murdoch Books UK
Ormond House, 26–27 Boswell Street,
    London WC1N 3JZ
Phone: +44 (0) 20 8785 5995
murdochbooks.co.uk
info@murdochbooks.co.uk

A catalogue record for this
book is available from the
National Library of Australia

A catalogue record for this book is available from the British Library

ISBN 978 1 92261 670 8

Cover illustrations, design and text design by Design by Committee
Internal illustrations by Matt Golding

Typeset by Midland Typesetters
Printed and bound by C&C Offset Printing Co. Ltd., China

We acknowledge that we meet and work on the traditional lands of the Cammeraygal
people of the Eora Nation and the Wurundjeri people of the Kulin Nation, and we pay
our respects to their elders past, present and future.

10 9 8 7 6 5 4 3 2 1

CONTENTS

FIRST THINGS FIRST

A baby enters the world. Why is no urgent warning provided about the language task to come? If the child is destined to speak English, will no one take the time amid the whole birth/mess/squalling situation to point out that *defuse* and *diffuse* are easily mixed up, that apostrophes are known to bite, that a dangling modifier is not a reference to the time Michael Jackson suspended his baby son over a hotel railing? Where's the advice about why *psychedelic* has a *p* in it? What about a gentle caution that hardly anyone outside art-exhibition circles can remember whether *biannual* or *biennial* means twice yearly so you might as well avoid them both from the start?

It could be argued that the doctors, midwives, parents and other attendees have too much else on their minds to be worrying about imparting wisdom on the importance of getting *there*, *they're* and *their* right. Further squalling could be on the way.

Shock, awe, exhaustion, euphoria and/or a strong desire for a tuna sandwich may have set in. Conspiracy theorists may be certain the newborn is being deprived of information because to know the difference between *eek* and *eke* is to know that all grown-ups have an implanted microchip, one that enables control by polka-dot snail-like creatures from the planet Zygflp.

The other explanation for the lack of language enlightenment is that all attempts are futile, as the bawling bundle of joy won't understand a thing. A reasonable argument. Ah, but the time will come, and it won't be far off ...

* * *

Having started life as a bawling bundle of joy, I progressed at more or less the usual pace to intermittent bawler and occasional articulator of the Australian version of English. By the age of four, I could chatter away and ruin any good movie or TV show for my fellow viewers by making inconvenient demands for plot explanations. Having a late bedtime and not being restricted to kiddie fare made it understandable that there were many questions that just had to be asked.

I was aware when sent off to school from the age of almost five (something about someone having decided that education is a personal and societal good), that learning to read and write was going to be part of the deal. Any hopes of being able to advance through primary, secondary and tertiary education absorbed solely in finger-painting lessons were soon left lying in the gutter near the football oval. For no particular reason, the five-year-old version of me feared I would never get the hang of reading. I was wrong about that. And it turned out reading and writing had the potential to be not only useful but also engrossing, thought-provoking and fun, instruction manuals for electrical goods aside.

There are many routes to becoming a journalist. I took one of them, having been influenced by a childhood spent watching way too many TV news bulletins and current affairs shows back to back. If there was a newspaper lying around, which there always was, it would be read. Perhaps as an antidote to all those TV news bulletins and current affairs shows (I can reliably inform you it's a scary world out there), newspaper columns written by humorists were judged particularly appealing. Apart from the rare odd job (a day as a movie extra, a shift or two spent checking numbers to do with shipping and learning what a bill of lading was), word wrestling of the newspaper and news website variety is what I've been up to, having leapt into the fray during a century not all that long ago.

I've been a news reporter and a feature writer, but most of my time has been spent as a subeditor (aka desk editor or producer) working in daily news, the area where deadlines are at their least merciful. I'm one of those behind-the-scenes people whose job it is to get words ready to be published online and in print. We're polishers. We strive to hunt down errors and inconsistencies, and to improve clarity. We grapple with the grammar. We nip and tuck or go in up to our elbows for radical surgery if required. We smooth out wrinkles of the written variety – no Botox needed. We provide a fresh eye that might see a better way to phrase something or to spark reader interest. Skilled subs will also know when to refrain from application of mitts and leave a fine piece of work well enough alone. We're genetically programmed to like witty headlines, and with luck even manage to write a few. With even more luck, they're applied to stories for which they're appropriate.

This book is about playing nicely by current conventions of standard English. It contains myth-dismantling, a dash of historical context, a writing tip here and there, and a confusion-removal service. Everyone has their bugbears. You'll probably find a few of yours here. In the belief that venting is healthy, I'll throw in a few of my own, too, while trying to keep arbitrariness to manageable proportions.

I've worked on in-house newsroom style guides and sent out regular rambles to my colleagues about what we get up to with language. This has meant much pondering and reading about how English goes about its daily business. Some confirmed suspicions: it's messy and ever changing. Attempts to apply logic are likely to cause excruciating forehead pain, and not everything thought of as a rule stands up to scrutiny. *Convention* is a much better word than *rule* anyway. Yes, we have our settled ways, our accepted spellings and expected punctuation and syntax, but this language called English is devoid of a grand body laying down laws that if breached will lead to incarceration somewhere dark, dank and lacking access to Instagram.

Different conventions exist for different settings. In certain circles, inserting fewer than four exclamation marks in a row into a text message will leave those on the receiving end fearful for the health of the sender. Mucking up *practise* and *practice* in a news article will be enough to confirm for some readers that standards have declined to such a point that the end of civilisation will be upon us by dinnertime. Reporters and subeditors do hate when we muck up our *practises* and *practices*, by the way. We also hate when imperfect spellcheckers don't save us, or their good advice has been neglected. Think of me as looking sheepish on everyone's behalf while apologising and muttering about accidents and deadlines. We're glad that readers care.

If we take a broader view, it's clear that complaints and fears about language decline have always been with us. Everything seems sped up these days, and that's disconcerting, but we appear to have been complaining about decline for as long as we've had the means to complain. It's a wonder we've any language left given the perceived level of erosion.

The more you look at it the more you realise language is always in flux. The title of this book, *Writely or Wrongly*, isn't meant to suggest rights and wrongs set in stone for eternity. The *wrong* it refers to lies in that notion. If we're to be able to communicate effectively, we need conventions and an ability to know what's appropriate in different circumstances. Anyone insisting that the word *phone* means a type of chair or full stops belong in the middle of every word isn't going to get far at this point in language and phone evolution. But pedantry and unnecessary straitjackets are not the answer.

I'm all for locking unhelpful so-called rules away in a box marked "Wrong beyond redemption" along with misconceptions that hinder good writing, whether it be a piece of journalism, a short story, an essay, a novel, a blog or a CV. Pointing out these things isn't to take an "anything goes" approach. Far from it. Shooting off a quick message to a friend is one thing. Applying a more formal standard elsewhere smooths the way to broader communication and shows that writers care and have put thought into what they have to say.

A decent grasp of how to play nicely can also open the door to effective rule bending or breaking. Let's keep our CVs and formal reports on the straight and narrow, but literary experimentation can be a wonderful thing elsewhere. It's not as if great writers haven't been mucking around for centuries, getting gloriously muddy in the playground and creating whole new games. It does help if we mere mortals know when we're going too far though. Former US Republican vice-presidential candidate Sarah Palin didn't do herself or the language any favours in 2010 when she justified her blending of *refute* and *repudiate* to come up with *refudiate* by tweeting that Shakespeare liked to coin new words too. Yes, he did. But ...

PS: For all the many words I encountered in my school days, grammar terms were scarce. I learnt the basics of what nouns, pronouns, verbs and adjectives were, but along with millions of others, I don't remember diving in much deeper than that. The definition of a preposition? Maybe. Compound predicate, split infinitive, participle, modal auxiliary? Certainly not. Maybe a pronoun here and there. Pluperfect tense, predicate nominative? Stop swearing. I've read about them since, but keeping my distance still comes naturally. The odd grammar term will appear in the following pages, but not unless it's on its best behaviour. No muscling in without explanation, no hogging the limelight.

PPS: Readers may find slip-ups on my part. They're deliberate, added as a sort of non-treasure hunt anyone can undertake. OK, they're not deliberate, but I'd be obliged if you think they are anyway.

BLURP
RIBBIT
SNORT
GRUNT
ER HUM... AS UNACCUSTOMED TO THE ENGLISH LANGUAGE AS I AM...

CHAPTER 1

A THING OR TWO THAT GOT US HERE

I once had a rapid-paced night at the theatre in which all of Shakespeare's plays were shoehorned into an hour and a half or so. That the frantic actors up on the stage didn't collapse from exhaustion is a testament to their stamina. If it felt as if no time had passed between the witches' cauldron bubbling in *Macbeth* and Juliet wherefore art thou-ing that Romeo bloke, the simple explanation was that no time *had* passed. That's what this chapter reminds me of – much ramming, cramming, omission and minimising of significant events. See that intricacy over there? Let's jettison it. However, even in this sped-up modern age it's nice to have a little context about the linguistic journey we've been on. Let's prepare ourselves for a prehistoric grunt or two, an invasion here, an invasion there, the rise of powerful forces and the fall of powerful forces, and off we go.

Typical bawling bundles of joy deprived of a warning about *defuse* and *diffuse* and *biennial* and *biannual* manage to pick up in a few short years and with a minimum of fuss a huge amount about how language works. They don't need formal instruction in how sentences are put together to be able to start talking. Their brains, voice-box paraphernalia and social interaction will get them there. Off they'll go in at least one language, speeding from baby babble to lucid, grammatical pestering of parents for ice cream.

No classroom attendance is required to learn that repeating in English "I want ice cream" seven times in the space of one minute is the way to take delivery of a scoop of strawberry scrumptiousness. "Ice want cream I" may get young humans there, but not without the risk of delayed gratification as parents slow on the uptake deploy their deciphering skills. Subject (*I*), verb (*want*) object (*ice cream*) is the way to go in a simple English sentence, and three-year-olds have twigged to this and gone that way with great success. The oldest *Homo sapiens* remains found so far have been dated to 300,000 years ago, and earlier types of humans were pottering about long before that. It should be noted, though, that it is only in recent times that our offspring have been able to ask for ice cream with any reasonable expectation of receiving any.

Linguists, anthropologists, psychologists, cognitive scientists, evolutionary biologists and others have expended a great deal of energy trying to determine how and when our way with language came about. Have they agreed? Hah! Is it mostly innate, or is it mostly cultural? Did it appear relatively suddenly during human evolution, or did it grow out of primitive ways ancestors of humans communicated? Writing dates back only a few thousand years, so no one was keeping notes. Nor can we expect soundbites from prehistoric times to be dug out of the ground and put on museum display next to the Stone Age equivalent of a cutlery set.

So murky has the situation been that in 1866 the Linguistic Society of Paris famously banned discussion about the origin of language, having decided it was a mystery that couldn't be solved. This attitude had a dampening effect on discussion and research for many decades, but you can't keep a good inquiring mind down. Such minds have looked into the mystery and continue to do so.

Language ponderers of the 1800s may not be up there with the theorists and researchers behind modern scholarly thought, but some entertaining ways have been devised to categorise the speculation of their day as to where our first words came from. The bow-wow theory, the pooh-pooh theory, the yo-he-ho theory and their relatives can go ahead and take a bow in recognition of their efforts, even if they have all had holes shot in them one way or another. The bow-wow theory related to the idea that speech arose from the copying of sounds heard in nature, particularly animal sounds. The pooh-pooh theory put the focus on automatic vocal outpourings such as gasps, groans and laughter. Did it all really begin with an ancient human letting out an "Aargh!" after stubbing an ancient human toe on an ancient non-human rock? Maybe not, said the yo-he-ho school of thought, which suggested grunts and chants people used to co-ordinate their actions when working together might have held the key.

However it happened, once on our way, off we went in thousands of directions. The language data resource Ethnologue put the number of languages in use as of 2022 at more than 7,000, although many had few speakers and about 40 per cent were endangered. Tens of thousands of dialects exist, not that distinguishing between a language and a dialect is clear-cut. According to one old quip about languages and power, a language is a dialect with an army and a navy to back it up.

Counting native and non-native speakers around the world, Ethnologue listed English as top of the language pops with about 1.5 billion speakers, followed by Mandarin Chinese. Exclude non-native speakers and English was ranked third behind Mandarin and Spanish. The English speakers aren't all speaking English to the same degree, of course. Nor are they all speaking the same English. Variations are everywhere, and Australian English is called Australian English for a reason, mate.

Just as we praise the versatility, liveliness and expressiveness that English brings to communication, we're within our rights to take time to be rankled. *Inflammable* and *flammable* mean the same thing, and *tomb*, *bomb* and *comb* don't rhyme. Are you rankled yet? We have our *-able* words, our *-ible* words and an "*i* before *e* except after *c*" rule that mocks us. Nothing less is to be expected from a language that has been mutating for so many centuries and has borrowed (nay, habitually snaffled, some would say) so much from so many.

It's not that English has a monopoly on messiness, idiosyncrasy and complexity; language is a tricky business. Modern English is a mix of early Germanic dialects, French, Latin, Greek, Italian, Indian languages, Arabic and hundreds of other tongues that have done their bit to shape what we have today. Having been around for so long, having changed so much and having absorbed so much from elsewhere, how could it not be complex?

I for one am grateful we modern-day English deployers have been spared having to assign grammatical genders to objects.

Old English treated nouns as masculine, feminine or neuter, but pretty much apart from the odd ship we might call a *she*, we throw in an *it* and feel content with a job well done. I can barely ask for a croissant in French. The thought of trying to learn whether that book on the coffee table is masculine and the *serviette de table* that's fallen to the floor and been trampled on is feminine horrifies me. Putting French in the shade, the West African language Fula has about 20 genders and add-on complexity as to how they're used. Perhaps that trampled-upon French table napkin is a thing of beauty after all.

Unperturbed about the linguistic fallout their tree-change adventure would bring, Germanic-language-speaking tribespeople (the Angles, Saxons, Jutes, Frisians and others) arrived in Britain from the 5th century onwards. They gained dominion over most of the island; we gained Old English, not that it would get the last word though. It's largely gobbledygook to us today even though stalwarts included in our basic vocabulary – such as *a*, *about*, *child*, *our* and *never* – date back to it. Starting in the late 8th century, along came the Vikings, who couldn't help but leave behind some Old Norse as they went about their more assertive daily activities. From Old Norse we ended up with friendly words such as *freckle*, *egg* and *cake*, as well as the more Viking stereotypical *berserk* and *ransack*.

William the Conqueror did his own invading from Normandy in 1066, and Old English gradually shifted into Middle English. The Anglo-Norman style of French reigned among the ruling class while the common folk raised on assorted dialects of English carried on doing the everyday things common folk did, with the down-to-earth vocabulary to match. It took 300 years for England to have a king who spoke English as his mother tongue. Words from the Norman vocabulary were influential in areas such as politics, the arts, law, scholarship and religion. As a result, we have *parliament, judge, jury, majesty, leisure, grammar* and thousands of other familiar examples. The wealthy should be thankful for *mansion*, otherwise they would have to call their housing style of choice something else that might not sound as impressive.

English was nothing if not a tough and dogged fighter, and it came to reassert itself as enthusiasm for French faded. It survived invasion – it adopted, adapted, mingled, spread, persisted and here we are. The influence of religion and heightened interest in Latin and Greek, the rise of the printing press and literacy, the growth of trade, the Industrial Revolution, colonialism and American cultural power all played huge parts in shaping the language.

If you consider it chaotic now, when William Caxton set up the first printing press in London in the 15th century there were no guides to spelling, punctuation and the rest of this grammar business to help in cleaning up the shambles with which he was confronted. The diversity of dialects added greatly to his problems. Realising it wouldn't be at all bad for business to have a potential readership who could find his books intelligible, Caxton, whose publications included Chaucer's *The Canterbury Tales*, played a key role in standardising the language. The dialect of London and its environs, home to prestige and power, would dominate, although standard English approaching what we're familiar with today still had several centuries of developing to do.

Before Caxton, scribes of variable skill copied manuscripts out by hand, often adding errors as they went. Words could be spelt dozens of ways. Melvyn Bragg, in his book *The Adventure of English*, says the word *she* appeared around the traps in more than 60 permutations. No subeditors were available at the time to exterminate 59 of them.

Understanding why English spelling is still oh so peculiar oh so often doesn't lie only in appreciating the number of words that have been absorbed from other languages and the way Old English and French spelling collided. Having an alphabet with 26 letters to represent a language with more than 40 distinct sounds was never going to help. In Caxton's time and beyond, printers and typesetters had a lot of guessing to do. They also made mistakes that stuck. Some of the typesetters of yore came from the European mainland and, lacking guidance and familiarity with English, can be forgiven for throwing in a spelling or two that worked just fine at home. The linguist David Crystal, in his book *Spell it Out: The Curious, Enthralling and Extraordinary Story of English Spelling*, mentions how Flemish typesetters injected the silent *h* into *ghost*. Where they came from, it was a *gheest* that did spooking duty. As well, typesetters were paid by the line, giving them a fine incentive to make words longer than they had to be. Throw in some more *e*'s? Why not? We must live with the consequences.

Look to events under way from the latter years of the Middle English period and you will find another part of the explanation for spelling's wayward tendencies. Now is the time for finger-pointing at the much-debated and much-studied Great Vowel Shift. A series of pronunciation changes from the 15th century or earlier that continued for more than 200 years, this did much to alter how English sounded, particularly its long vowels. Spellings were becoming more fixed, but rhymes and written accounts from the time show pronunciation to have been on the move. *Wife* was previously pronounced *weef*, for instance, and *mice* as *mees*. These days we pronounce the *i* in *decline* and the *i* in *routine* differently, reflecting that letter's varied history. *Boot* once sounded more like *boat*. Today the *oo* of *food* is pronounced differently to the *oo* of *stood*, which is different to the *oo* of *blood*. All three would have once sounded akin to *goad*.

As well, some consonants were simplified or made silent, which in the case of *knight* and other *kn-* words was a good thing. K-nights cutting k-notted rope with k-nives are hard to take seriously. And it's a relief to be able to stay away from their k-nobbly k-nees.

The trouble with all this language shifting is that what might have worked as phonetic spelling in much of Middle English no longer matched pronunciation. We still have spellings from that period, but how we say so many words changed. Oops!

CHAPTER 2

THINGS TO STAY CALM ABOUT: RULES THAT AREN'T RULES

The French have their Académie Française to act as an official language watchdog and authority on matters of usage, vocabulary and grammar. It's been around since the 1630s, and its members are known as "immortals", an unrealistically optimistic designation if ever there was one. The British media enjoy poking fun at the efforts of the French body and the French government to keep words from across the Channel and the United States at bay. Not even online gaming terms avoid scrutiny. *E-sports*? Certainly not. *Jeu video de competition*, if you please. An online *streamer*? *Joueur-animateur en direct*. Still the English invaders keep coming, and the French populace decides on its own terms, despite the efforts of the academy and bureaucrats, whether to welcome them.

Dozens of other countries have language academies. The Swedish Academy, for instance, works for the "purity, vigour and majesty" of Swedish. My knowledge of matters Swedish extending not much further than ABBA and a four-letter acronym associated with flat-pack furniture and bargain-price storage solutions, I have no opinion on the academy's success rate but suspect purity maintenance is not for the faint-hearted.

Despite talk going back centuries about setting up an English equivalent, English has no official academy producing dictionaries and attempting to lay down the law. It's just us and the conventions we've arrived at unconsciously, or through people seeking to establish order and sometimes being successful enough to have large numbers of other people heed them. I'm a rule follower by nature. I spend my working life following standard procedure with standard English as best I can discern it. Some days my rule-following volume dial is set to 11 (reference to key cultural moment from the mockumentary *This Is Spinal Tap* intended). However, I don't see the need to fuss about nonsensical so-called rules that don't help communication but have lingered despite numerous efforts to debunk them.

Self-appointed 18th- and 19th-century arbiters produced a flood of grammar books as they sought to grab the language by the scruff of the neck and tell it how to get its act together. We're still influenced by the edicts and opinions of old. Some were useful to clear communication and establishing sensible order; some were eccentric and perverse, seemingly devised on a whim or based on the principle that whatever people do naturally must be wrong. Generations of schoolchildren were taught the helpful and the unhelpful by teachers who had canes and knew how to use them. It's a relief to report we've moved on in so many ways. However, mention of the word *grammar* can still bring to mind folklore that somewhere along the line hardened into something more, ably assisted by decrees devised without attention to how language works.

Split when it suits

The lucky among us get through life without ever having heard of split infinitives. My ignorance lasted into adulthood. Then I vaguely became aware of an issue but didn't understand what it was. Then I came upon the "rule" and began to fear split infinitives because a lot of other people knew about the "rule" and didn't take kindly to it being broken. Adherence seemed the easy way out, even though the more I read, the more I learnt that the edict had been widely dismissed by language experts and usage guides. I'll give it points for persistence, but on my low-compliance days I'll ignore it and consider I'm doing my bit to aid its demise. There's so much splitting going on in the modern world that I'm in good company.

So what is a split infinitive? Deep sigh. It's about taking a *to* and sticking another word or phrase between it and the verb it goes with. *To slowly abandon, to incessantly decry, to permanently delete*, consider your infinitives split. Rare is the usage guide published since *Star Trek* became a hit that hasn't mentioned "*to boldly go* where no man has gone before". Just to show how much I can be a traditionalist, I've now mentioned it too. What makes those examples hideous? Nothing. Victorian-era dogmatists and a few others who beat them to the argument decided otherwise for dubious and tiresome reasons, and their pronouncements took hold. Perhaps they had a good marketing team.

Irish playwright George Bernard Shaw was a man with strong opinions about a lot of subjects. It's a shame he missed the Twitter era, but he had other ways to censure, and he wasn't going to hold back about his right to infinitely split. Fulminating in a 19th-century letter to a newspaper against an anti-splitter in its ranks, he wrote:

> *There is a busybody on your staff who devotes a lot of his time to chasing split infinitives. Every good literary craftsman splits his infinitives when the sense demands it. I call for the immediate dismissal of this pedant. It is of no consequence whether he decides to go quickly or quickly to go or to quickly go. The important thing is that he should go at once.*

American-British novelist Raymond Chandler was another writer prone to touchiness at tampering with his splitting:

> *when I split an infinitive, God damn it, I split it so it will remain split.*

The thunderings of Shaw and Chandler aside (and they are far from the only famous writers to like a good split), a sound argument against avoiding split infinitives at all costs is that doing so can lead to ambiguity and/or a tortured result, and we can all agree that the world already has enough of those. Splitting comes naturally to us; it fits with many of our idioms, and no aliens encountered by the crew of the starship USS *Enterprise* have seen cause to complain. Not even Mr Spock has complained, and he's a creature of logic.

Should you find it more elegant to leave the *to* next to the verb, all will be well most of the time. Should you feel that people will think you're more careful if you avoid splitting, that's fine. But consider these: *expected to triple more than in two years* and *expected more than to triple*. Performing a neat split and rewording those to read *expected to more than triple* is the way out of their problem. *Regularly to reject doing housework* sounds as awkward as an elephant trying to balance on a coffee table. *To reject regularly doing housework* lands us in ambiguity territory. Is the rejecting regular or is it regular housework that's being rejected? *To reject doing housework regularly* suggests that irregular housework is not frowned upon. *To regularly reject* has a satisfying flow and makes it clear that the rejecting is regular. By the way, do the elephant a favour. You know how. Get it off the coffee table.

No leg to stand on

Prepositions are harmless. These innocent fellas are part of the team: *at*, *before*, *behind*, *on*, *in*, *off*, *up*, *with*, *after*. They enjoy hanging out in front of nouns for the most part, expressing a relationship between them and something else. They tell us a lot about where and when: *on the slide*, *under the mattress*, *after the debacle*, *before the apocalypse*. They're used before our hard-working pronouns too. The trouble starts when we get to our habit of sending them scurrying to the ends of sentences. Surely no offence can be taken from the cute little *on* that's about to appear:

> *Get Jamila's guinea pig off that coffee table the elephant's trying to balance on.*

The 17th-century English poet John Dryden would have been offended by that even without the benefit of online outrage generators to fuel his umbrage. Dryden may not have come up with the non-rule that sentences shouldn't end with a preposition, but his disapproval of ones that did helped lead to its spread. His thinking may have been part of an obsession certain influential people had in those days with trying to make English work in the way Latin worked, conveniently ignoring how

everyone else used English and the fact that Latin, while important to English, happened to be, and let's be blunt about this, a
different language.

In the 20th century, Winston Churchill was renowned not
only for his leadership during the dark days of World War II
and a cigar habit so strong that he would have fought anti-
smoking campaigners on the beaches to defend it. His
purported foray into the battle over preposition placement also
became the stuff of legend. Just as it's hard to ignore *to boldly go*
in any post–*Star Trek* discussion of split infinitives, Churchill
is forever being mentioned as a prime opponent of the non-rule
about prepositions. While we can be sure of what Captain Kirk
uttered, we're proof-deprived as to whether Churchill ever did
say: "This is the kind of arrant pedantry up with which I will
not put." I feel confident in insisting he would not have tried
to ask Hitler for his opinion, but not at all confident about
the identity of the actual author of that line. As with so many
historical quotations, getting to the bottom of who really said
what when is like trying to persuade a lion that eating you will
give it indigestion: you're likely to fail and end up in a dark place
with lots of unidentifiable muck around you within the belly of
a disagreeable beast.

Regardless of the quip's dodgy backstory and criticism it
doesn't technically work as an illustration of the issue at hand
anyway, it does make a point up with which we really should
put. Avoiding ending a sentence with a preposition can tie you

in knots. Using a strong word at the far end of a sentence rather than a puny preposition will often make for a punchier overall result, but that's a matter of style rather than grammar. Burning someone at the stake for doing otherwise will only contribute to global warming for no reason.

But why not start a sentence with a *but* or an *and*?

And in further non-breaking news, it's OK to begin sentences with linking words such as *and*, *but* and *so*. I picked up somewhere along the line that to do so was to be condemned if not to hell then to the seedy caravan park next door. Hell no – not at all. *And* can be found at the start of sentences going back to Anglo-Saxon times. *But* has been the sentence-opener of choice for all manner of heavyweight writers. Overdoing it creates monotony, but that's a different matter.

And, *but* and *so* are part of the conjunction crew. They're co-ordinating conjunctions, those words that happily connect equally important ideas. FANBOYS is the acronym commonly used to help people remember seven hard workers in this group. Although male Whovians, Trekkies and connoisseurs of the Marvel Cinematic Universe have been found to be regular users of co-ordinating conjunctions, FANBOYS in the language sense represents *for*, *and*, *nor*, *but*, *or*, *yet*, *so*. It doesn't hurt to know this, but any suggestion that such knowledge is vital for daily living is to be shouted down. The main thing is that sentences are varied, variety being the spice of you know what. Should more formality than a mere *and* or *but* be wanted, words such as *however*, *furthermore* or *moreover* are standing by for sentence-starting duty.

That which is OK

Take a look at the following sentences:

The porridge that Goldilocks wolfed down was just right.
The porridge which Goldilocks wolfed down was just right.
The porridge, that Goldilocks wolfed down, was just right.

It's easy to see the third sentence needs to head off to rehab. The way *that* is used makes a rapid detox in order. To resolve the problem, *which* needs to replace the badly positioned *that*, which doesn't belong after the comma. The clause it's part of is a nonessential clause, one that should take a *which*. It offers extra information that can be removed and still leave a sensible sentence:

The porridge was just right. Oh, and by the way, she wolfed it down.

In the first two sentences, the information that the bowl of porridge being discussed is the one that was wolfed down by Goldilocks, as opposed to the porridge spurned for being too hot or too cold, is essential to the meaning. It is presented in a comma-free essential clause. It is sometimes said *which* is wrong in such cases, a view up with which you do not need to put. *Which* or *that* may be applied, although *that* is more prevalent in speech. Oft-cited 20th-century usage guide granddaddy Henry Watson Fowler thought it would aid lucidity and ease if *that* won the battle in written English, but he acknowledged in the 1920s that neither most nor the best writers were paying that idea any attention. Keep *that* out of the third example on the previous page. *That* or *which* will do in the first and second. Meanwhile, as an intruder in the three bears' home, Goldilocks should have ditched her sense of entitlement and been grateful she found any porridge at all.

An alternative point of view

The notion is out there that *alternative* is appropriate only with a choice of two things. Pick up this idea, carry it to a nearby bin and deposit it deep inside. Make sure it isn't a recycling bin, as we want this to go straight to landfill. You may comfortably have three or more *alternatives*, so go ahead. There's more to be said about *alternative*, but I'm saving that for when it catches up with its pal, *alternate*, in Chapter 8.

Not one justification

Were you taught that *none* has to be accompanied by a singular verb because it means *not one*? That would leave you with a sentence of this persuasion:

None of them is *watching as the language traditions head out the door.*

Although *none* comes from an Old English word meaning *not one*, it's been used with a plural or a singular verb for about 1,000 years, depending on the context and the emphasis wanted. That's a millennium's worth of plural treatment. Quite a tradition there, and one that hasn't headed out the door yet.

Between a rock and ...

Should you meet on your travels people who insist *between* must not be used unless talking about two things or people and that *among* must be used for more than that, do not trust them. They're peddling a myth. *Between* cries out for use if you're dealing with two things that are clearly separate:

There's a connection between untrustworthy acquaintances and wallet endangerment. Between you and me, I'd leave your wallet at home.

However, it's also fine to use *between* for more than two things that are separate, particularly if those things are equal:

Between you, me and the person bugging your phone, these new acquaintances of yours sound as dodgy as that interior decorator who wanted you to line your kitchen ceiling with fake fur.

Among comes into the picture when the focus is on things or people collectively and indistinctly:

Among some out-there schools of interior decorating thought, fake fur on ceilings is considered state of the art.
There is no doubt among mainstream interior decorators that kitchen ceilings and fake fur should never meet.

* * *

It can't be easy to be devoted to non-rules in the 21st century. To be faced with attacks on edicts held dear or drummed in many moons ago isn't going to help at the end of a long day of queasiness induced by the discovery that a dear friend has ended a sentence with a preposition. However, dictates that are of suspect origin and impede communication deserve to be questioned. Numerous language experts have long given them short shrift. Doing so is not the same as calling for the abandonment of all standards. It's helpful standards we want. As for the super-sticklers, they've always had a hard time. For all the comfort it can provide at the height of a split infinitive outbreak, nostalgia for some sort of golden age of English when everyone did as they were told is based on fantasy.

CHAPTER 3

THAT WRITING THING: ARE WE CLEAR?

Any writing that goes beyond a reminder to pick up bread, rapid-fire online posts and cheating using artificial intelligence takes thought. Speech flows naturally, but writing falls into the effort category even when the advice is to write as you would speak. This is something with which journalists, internet contributors, novelists, essay producers, report authors, instruction manual creators, lesson devisers and everyday scribblers have to contend. If it weren't a fact of life, we wouldn't have the saying that writers like having written rather than writing. Nor would someone have devised procrastination. Excuse me while I go and tidy up a cutlery drawer ... I'm back, and the drawer's looking fine, thanks.

We go to the effort in order to get a message across, but confusion gets in the way. So much more needs to be thought about than whether a few grammar conventions have been followed.

Is logic anywhere to be seen? Has the point run off when no one was looking? Has the ambiguity quota (zero unless for deliberate creative purposes) been breached? Is the language impenetrable and/or sleep-inducing? It's going to take more than the odd tip to turn someone into the next Margaret Atwood, Ernest Hemingway, Peter Carey or Virginia Woolf. But there are basics that help us all in the everyday business of clear communication. They apply even if the noble pursuit of elegant and engaging writing isn't reducible to five rules stuck on a fridge, especially if it's a small fridge or one already overcrowded with magnets.

Plain is good

Not even in formal contexts is the attitude helpful that only the longest, most obscure words and phrases will do the trick. The aim is to communicate clearly, not to show that the author has been on an unguided trip around a thesaurus and brought back enough souvenirs to fill four suitcases. No law exists against using *prognosticate* instead of *predict*, *incommodious* over *uncomfortable* or *sedulous* for *diligent*. If you're being creative and a touch of floweriness or mock floweriness helps, they're at your disposal. Taking the side of plain English is not to suggest it be used like a straitjacket. A more unusual word can brighten things up or hit the right note at the right moment, but there's a difference between that and sounding pompous or being woefully obscure.

Start is more natural than *commence*; *heading north* is more natural than *proceeding in a northerly direction*. Writing in a natural way isn't talking down to readers. Using only the fanciest of words in the belief they'll be evidence of care and consideration risks leaving readers carefully considering whether to give up on reading and do something else. I've only just discovered *sedulous* and expect I'll never type it again unless forced to by someone holding a tomato sauce bottle to my head and threatening to squeeze it. No moisture shed from ocular organs about that, and un-Australian hatred of tomato sauce admitted without shame or fear of citizenship being revoked.

It's with good reason that journalists are encouraged to stick to *said* when someone being quoted has *uttered, postulated* or *declared* something of note. As a profession, we're well practised at keeping *vocalised* and *posited* away from readers. We're not shunning those words to save on ink or keystrokes. An unadorned *said* does the job. It's short. It's clear. It doesn't jar or otherwise get in the way. Fiction writers are within their rights to mix things up a little, but much advice for them also falls into the "stick to an unobtrusive *said*" category. American writer Elmore Leonard, whose novels include *Get Shorty*, was a *said* man through and through. Using it unnecessarily sentence after sentence in quick succession will be a tedious turn-off, but a *he orated* followed by a *she burbled* followed by a *they avouched* is not anyone's idea of an improvement.

Spare us the jargon

Jargon is a special type of anything-but-plain language. Such is its ubiquity and the extent to which it makes writing unclear and me grumpy that I'm giving it its own special section. Academia, business, the armed forces, the law, medicine – they're jargon breeders all.

We can't expect the world to get by without jargon. Anyone who doesn't think planet Earth is a complex place in need of specialist words hasn't been paying attention in recent millennia. A geneticist writing to a colleague about *haplotypes* should feel free to do so. Does it clarify things if I say a classic example of these is the cluster of HLA alleles in the major histocompatibility complex? No? Oh well. The experts are writing in a common language, using a shortcut for something geneticists know about. They don't want to have to define their terms at every mention. We shouldn't make them when they're among their own kind. If physicists in the privacy of their own academic journals want to have their *Pauli exclusion principle* and *adiabatic processes*, that's fine. Just keep them away from me.

So much for jargon with a positive role. Research suggests that elsewhere insecurity, a desire for status and showing off keep people reaching for the language of the in-crowd over ordinary words that will leave a general readership content. Jargon may come easily, but efforts to avoid making things harder to read than they have to be should be applauded, even in academic or technical reports. Psychologist, linguist and author Stephen Pinker writes in his book *The Sense of Style: The Thinking Person's Guide to Writing in the 21st Century* that scientists who replace *murine model* with *rats and mice* are no less scientific for doing so and that a surprising amount of jargon can be done away with to no ill effect.

Yes, legalese can help ensure language precision on weighty matters of the law, but that argument only gets us so far. It isn't only laypeople who view the plain-English contract as a thing of beauty, and lawyers preferring *locus delicti* over *crime scene* might want to consider whether they've created a crime scene of their own. Although there's one Latin term that's acceptable to describe overuse of jargon: the *status quo*.

Leveraged any synergies in the past fortnight? If so, it can be assumed you're familiar with business jargon. As we *have the bandwidth*, let's *grab some low-hanging fruit, circle back on that, reach out* to one another, toss around some thoughts on *core deliverables* and accept the *key learnings*. This kind of thing's deadening effect on writing is everywhere. If any form of jargon is at risk of taking over the world, it's the corporate variety. It develops for the reasons mentioned previously and will continue to do so. However, even the corporate world recognises it as a problem. It can leave workers feeling alienated and hinder communication from managers. Management consultants out there will help companies cure their jargonitis just as other management consultants are busy getting paid to come up with more jargon.

I like to think most of us use jargon innocently enough. But a further reason it exists is its usefulness when the aim is to confuse and obscure. Certain business folk and politicians have been known to see the benefit in confusion, obscurity and euphemism when trouble arises. Look no further for a way to blur the fact that jobs are being lost: put out a statement saying *operational efficiencies* are being created, *streamlining* is taking place, some *demising* of roles is required (thank a bank press release for that one), or a little *right-sizing* will make all well.

The joys of brevity

Many evenings in the newsroom I've heard a cry along the lines of: "They've done another Tolstoy!" It's not a compliment but a complaint from a colleague who has yet again picked up an online version of a story, one not constrained by space, only to find it too long for the real estate available in a physical newspaper. A trim is in order. In desperate circumstances, major surgery is needed in the minutes before the nightly print deadline slaps us about the face. A product that stretches would be a solution. Surely someone could devise a way to print newspapers on giant sheets of chewing gum for readers who prefer something they can hold rather than a website.

In the absence of the chewing-gum solution, squeezing stories into tight places in newspapers is unavoidable. But freedom from space constraints online and elsewhere isn't a licence to run wild. Tight writing says what needs to be said without wasting words. The thing is it's harder to write shorter than it is to write longer.

Getting the clutter out takes work. French 17th-century mathematician Blaise Pascal put it this way:

> *I didn't have time to write a short letter, so I wrote a long one instead.*

Our brains are content to use five words where one will do. Writing becomes bloated and clarity pays the price. The effort to be efficient in the first place or to go back and chop where chopping is needed is worth it. Here come some candidates for easy chopping:

on a monthly basis	*monthly*
on an hourly basis	*hourly*
to facilitate improvement	*help*
put an emphasis on	*emphasise*
at this point in time	*now*
gained entrance to	*entered*
in the wake of	*after*
very, very large	*large or, even shorter, big*
due to the fact that	*because*
by virtue of the fact that	*because*
because of the fact that	*because*
was of the opinion that	*thought*
engage in dialogue	*talk*

Remember there's someone on the receiving end

Thinking of readers is the polite thing to do. It's also crucial. Is a broad readership being aimed at or people with specialist knowledge? How much background will anyone need to work out what's happening? Could a sentence that's clear to the writer be read two ways by someone else? Readers have a lot else going on. It's inhuman, especially when there's a good movie waiting to be watched, to make them struggle through something that's shown them no consideration. I find myself in bugbear territory if faced with news reports that assume I've memorised a story on the same topic from the week before and don't need a recap. I want my recap. Even when those on the receiving end have no choice but to immerse themselves in a report for work, the thought that they're getting paid to plough on can only compensate for so much.

I wasn't impressed with a textbook for beginner Mandarin learners that plunged straight into telling readers that the *f* sound is a labio-dental voiceless fricative, although I was relieved to know *t* is merely an aspirated voiceless plosive. You can read all about these things on pages five and six. You'll have to wait until page 14 before you can say hello (*ni hao*).

Think outside the cliché box

They're as old as the hills, they can be as alike as two peas in a pod and if you play your cards right and go back to the drawing board you can ensure they suffer a death by a thousand cuts. The convenience of unoriginal, overused ideas and phrases that have long lost meaning and oomph keeps them in circulation. They started off as clever but now they're dull. These days, an online cliché checker can seek them out and destroy them for you, but the temptation to reach for them as a form of shorthand is strong when there is washing to be done, it's a dark and stormy night and the brain cells needed for literary inventiveness have gone to the Gold Coast for the weekend. I'm reluctant to quote American author and columnist William Safire's admonition on this subject: "Last but not least, avoid clichés like the plague." It's become a cliché about avoiding clichés, but now I've gone and quoted it and slapped myself on the wrist accordingly.

Abbreviate with caution

A favourite impenetrability destruction method of mine is to see how many unfamiliar abbreviations I can cut out of news stories. It's a little victory that brings disproportionate enjoyment. The alphabet soup may be cold and tasteless, but there's something about slurping it so that readers don't have to that creates a warm glow. It's not the familiar, commonly used abbreviations that are the problem. They can hold their heads up high, and here's to the UK, NASA, the CIA and Australia's dear ASIO. I'll even be charitable and throw in LOL. No one's complaining about the ABC (well, they are, but not because of the abbreviation). The FBI, ATMs and RSVP are fine.

Writing littered with unfamiliar abbreviations will only be a turn-off. If you're mentioning three committees, you may need to resort to abbreviations to distinguish them. If only one, name it and call it *the committee* thereafter. Should you need to tell a colleague that you sent a request to the Victorian Department of Environment, Land, Water and Planning, that colleague would be in your debt if you referred to it as *the department* at further mention and not DELWP. It's particularly impolite to subject anyone to a DELWP before breakfast.

A book of abbreviations put out by the British Ministry of Defence contains 402 (yes, 402) pages of them, each page having about 50 (yes, 50) entries. That's more than 20,000 (yes, 20,000) abbreviations in total. Does a whole department exist to invent them? Could not one or two be done without? The final entry is *ZZ*. It stands for *zig-zag*, although I think more of *snooze*. I found a UK Department for International Development document on abbreviations to do with resilience. It lists only 69 and may be required reading after perusing the Ministry of Defence's effort. Let us agree that if an unfamiliar abbreviation serves no good purpose, the only polite thing to do is put it out of everyone's misery.

Get your active gear out, but tone down the passive aggression

Active sentences deserve the praise they get. Journalists are taught from the start to favour them. Active voice injects vigour and is direct. It's on the side of clarity and lets a sentence say what it has to say in fewer words. Consider these two:

The Guatemala Steamers flattened all opponents in the extreme-ironing competition.
All opponents were flattened by the Guatemala Steamers in the extreme-ironing competition.

The active first sentence immediately puts the focus on the doer of the action, in this case the mighty Steamers. The subject of the sentence, the Steamers, performs the action of the verb *flattened* on the object of the sentence, the opponents. In the passive second sentence, the focus shifts to the receivers of the action. The doer, despite a fine achievement, has been unsportingly relegated to second place in the sentence hierarchy.

An email to a colleague along the lines of "You stole my yoghurt from behind the cos lettuce in the fridge" is likely to get the guilty party's panic response kicking in faster than the following wilted effort: "My yoghurt behind the cos lettuce in the fridge was stolen by you." The thief, the doer of the sentence, needs to be to the fore. While we're removing the passive voice, the lettuce can go too. The guilty party knows where the yoghurt was.

Having praised the active, it should be acknowledged that the passive voice is given an unjustly rough time. It has its part to play too. The second sentence of this section, "Journalists are taught from the start to favour [active sentences]", is passive. The person or thing doing the teaching is irrelevant and therefore not even in the sentence. You don't need to know what the teacher's name and job title are or the name of the book containing that advice. The passive is a standard part of how we express ourselves. The key is to use it appropriately. "Stonehenge has been rebuilt a month after careless tourists knocked it over" gets off to a passive start but has more impact than: "A local construction company rebuilt Stonehenge after careless tourists knocked it over."

Much academic writing uses the passive voice. Many journals encourage active voice, but there's a traditional school of thought that calls for taking the doer out of the picture, barring entry to *I* and *we*. Backers of this approach see the distancing effect and formality of the passive voice as promoting objectivity, or at least the appearance of it. The opposing school of thought supports the active voice as a way to make complex scientific and technical reports more readable. Let's just say balance is a wonderful thing.

One passive example I've come across used 55 words before a verb appeared. I'll spare you the sentence because there's

a mountain of technical jargon in those 55 words and I wouldn't want any of it to escape and infect the rest of this book, but the gist was someone absent from the sentence was examining something. It wasn't the 55-word wait per se for some verb action with the arrival of "are examined" that made the sentence grammatically passive, but it didn't help the cause of active communication. Such was the overwhelming feeling of passivity that an image of a doormat made from sloth fur came to mind. How nice it would have been if the sentence had at least started with a cheeky and active: "We examined ..."

The passive voice can also be used out of politeness to avoid unnecessarily singling someone out, or the purpose can be to obscure something that shouldn't be obscured. The politician who writes "mistakes were made" neglects to say who made them; the bureaucrat who writes "rules were broken" does not identify the rule breaker and may consider the world a better place for that. Treasurers who need to point out that taxes were raised last year but are not keen on saying they raised them know the beauty of turning to the passive. It's a tool that can be used for good or evil.

Read aloud but not too loudly

Much writing advice suggests reading out loud will help highlight problem areas and keep rhythm flowing nicely. It does help, but this approach comes with embarrassment when other people are around. Buy a sound-level meter. Try not to go far beyond about 30 decibels, which is the level of a whisper. Know that hearing damage is possible above about 80 decibels, lawnmower level, after two hours of exposure.

Take a break

It's amazing what a little distance from the written word will do. I've calmed down from my earlier jargon rant for a start. You could take a break by making a cup of coffee, dancing to a bit of Beyoncé, cleaning the bath or extracting carpet fluff from between your toes. If you're writing in an office, you'll have the coffee option even if deprived of the others. As well as serving the purposes of procrastinators everywhere, mental mini-breaks really do provide clarity. Something that seemed to make sense and have every appearance of a masterpiece at 12.20pm may be unmasked at 12.32pm as the feeble effort it always was. Coming back to written output with a fresh eye the next day, the next week or even the next month can also have wondrous results. The chance to do that is a luxury journalists at the pointy end of news gathering are deprived of; readers want their news now. There's comfort for journalists, though, in the thought that others are taking the time to refine their own writing by at least removing carpet fluff from their toes.

Full disclosure

Journalism is known for its own oft-criticised writing habit, a style that goes under the name of journalese. How often do parents consider themselves to have *lambasted* their three-year-old for deciding her dinner needs to be smeared over the wall? Have you decided lately to *ramp up* your efforts to get the cat to look at you without disdain? Is your vacuum cleaner *slated for implementation* any time soon? Are you and your partner planning *bilateral talks* about whose turn it is to wash the dishes *in the wake of* an *unprecedented* sink build-up? I fear that in some journalistic households, all of the above apply.

In an effort to make life sound more exciting, contrasts will be *stark*, big numbers will be *staggering*, waters will be *shark-infested*, omissions will be *glaring*, infernos will be *blazing* and Person A will have *slammed* Person B – again. This type of thing ends up as journalists' own form of jargon and cliché. Some newsrooms love it; some try to weed it out. Spellcheckers can be customised to flag the worst of it. Journalese can be inevitable in the tightest of print headlines. These are inhospitable places where space is inflexible and *axed*, *bid* and *row* are beloved for their brevity.

Deadline pressure and familiarity make it understandable, too, that writers reach into their trusty and rusty old toolkit when nothing more natural or original comes to mind. I take heart from the fact that scientists and other experts are now rarely lumbered with the journalese label of *boffins*. I had originally written "never lumbered", but Google had evidence to the contrary. We shouldn't give up hope though. A *boffin*-free planet is achievable and can only be a good thing for experts and the rest of us.

Words of wisdom that may or may not be from Mark Twain

My rummaging makes me confident the quotation below is from the man who created Tom Sawyer and Huckleberry Finn:

> *When you catch an adjective, kill it. No, I don't mean utterly, but kill most of them – then the rest will be valuable. They weaken when they are close together. They give strength when they are wide apart.*

The next quotation is plastered all over the internet as also being from Twain, but beware – the internet and the truth have been known to vary. Although Twain was a prolific producer of quotable quotes, he may also hold the record for the person whose name is most often attached to quotations not of his making. Regardless of its source, the suggestion below is a memorable one about getting rid of an overused word renowned for doing little to earn its keep:

> *Substitute* damn *every time you're inclined to write very; your editor will delete it and the writing will be just as it should be.*

LET'S EAT UNCLE MAURICE

CHAPTER 4

THINGS THAT
PUNCTUATE OUR LIVES

Punctuation marks do good things. I may grumble at times, but I like them overall. As long as they're not overused, there's something appealing about the way they look. They speed up my ability to find my way around, doing a lot without taking up much space. They come with routine operating procedures but sometimes leave room for considered discretion too. They inject rhythm, clarity and clues to tone of voice. What's more, most of them don't show off about it. A tiny dot appears and I settle in for a pause at the end of that basic unit of language we call a sentence.

As many an internet meme has noted, a tiny dot accompanied by a tail can be the difference between life and death. "Let's eat, Uncle Maurice" isn't the same as the cannibal's preferred version: "Let's eat Uncle Maurice." With the addition of a tadpole-shaped bit of ink or some carefully arranged pixels in the form of a comma, cannibalistic thoughts are dispelled, ambiguity has met its match and Uncle Maurice can sleep safely at night. Context is everything, of course. A knowledge of the dietary habits of the person making the dining suggestion might also have removed the ambiguity, but you can never be too careful – I'm on the comma's side.

If it's peace and quiet you're after, don't think a conversation about punctuation is the place to find refuge. People can get passionate about this sort of thing. In at least one notable case, rising passions led to bloodshed. It happened in 1837 in Paris. Two legal experts got their swords out in a dispute over whether a passage should be accompanied by a semicolon or a colon. Reports say the supporter of the semicolon was wounded in the arm, which raises the question of whether his opponent attempted to get in a couple of thrusts that led to a colon-like scar and post-traumatic stress disorder triggered at every sight thereafter of two dots in vertical alignment.

Fiction writers of an experimental bent, another passionate lot, have long been taken with the thought of doing unexpected things with punctuation. American writer Gertrude Stein once told a reporter: "Punctuation is necessary only for the feeble-minded." Mind you, this is a person who attracted the following headline in *The New York Times* in 1934: "Gertrude Stein Arrives and Baffles Reporters by Making Herself Clear".

The last line of James Joyce's *Ulysses* ends with a full stop. There's nothing startling about that. The famously startling thing is that readers will have a hard time finding any others among the 24,000 or so words that precede it in the novel's final episode – there's one that snuck in amid the stream of consciousness. I have read that a single comma dwells among those 24,000 words, although I failed to find it in the version where I went hunting. The rest of the 265,000-word book offers some comfort for those who need their daily dose of commas and full stops, but Joyce has other ways to be different, among them using dashes rather than quotation marks to introduce dialogue.

Cormac McCarthy, author of *No Country for Old Men* and *The Road*, is another fan of sparse punctuation, advising in an interview with Oprah Winfrey in 2007 against blotting pages with "weird little marks".

Arguing the cause of literary experimentation won't get the average journalist far should they submit work better suited to *Ulysses* than a 600-word news report on government scandal No. 72 for the year. Nor will such an argument help the average scientific report writer or work emailer. Even literary experimenters must feel relieved if instructions for putting up shelves or operating a steam mop use full stops and commas at closer than 2,000-word intervals. Trying to get a new gadget up and running is not the time to be arguing about the stylistic merits of the semicolon in paragraph five of an instruction booklet.

That's not to say that what we think of as standard punctuation arose from the start of our written journey. One of the earliest alphabetic writing systems, the Ugaritic alphabet, dating back to about the 14th century BC, used, albeit inconsistently, a small vertical wedge shape to divide words. Some others used a vertical line, a single dot in the middle of a line or a vertical row of two or three dots. In what strikes this modern reader as a great leap backwards, along came *scriptio continua.* RUNWORDSANDSENTENCESTOGETHERLIKETHIS WITHOUTBREAKS and, as the name suggests, you have *scriptio continua.* If you really must know where one word ends and another begins, or where a pause would be nice, work it out for yourself. It was a language development that brings to mind a restaurant where you not only have to do your own cooking, but you're forced to go out and buy the cutlery, greet yourself at the front door, lay the table and mop the floor after dinner.

Classical Greek took an extended trip down the *scriptio continua* path, and Classical Latin gave it a whirl too. It was a time when reading aloud to an audience was routine and the reader had time to rehearse and work out how to treat all that *continua.* The method also provided a saving in ink and papyrus (have you seen the price of papyrus lately?) and helped scribes working with stone save room. A frugal scribe was a fulfilled scribe.

Luckily for us and particularly for readers of *Ulysses,* the concept of spaces between words took off from the 7th century AD. Irish, Anglo-Saxon and German scribes, possibly annoyed about having to wrangle strings of spaceless and unfamiliar Latin, latched on to the idea. As various punctuation marks were devised over the centuries and faster, silent reading became the norm, responsibility for punctuating shifted from reader to writer, or at least to printer if the writer had little clue what to do, not that printers were too sure either. Some punctuation marks displayed formidable staying power; others – such as the percontation point, a reverse question mark for rhetorical questions – were soon flung onto history's discard pile, at least as far as English was concerned.

We're more sparing in our use of punctuation, especially commas, than were the literary lot of the 18th and 19th centuries. We have our differences about where particular commas should and shouldn't go and whether the semicolon is peculiar, but we also have our settled rules thrown in with our optional extras and confusions. Given that part of what I do at my place of gainful employment entails comma adding, subtracting and shuffling, I notice when they crop up in newsrooms in strange places. They may not lurk behind the coffee machine or leap out from under unsuspecting trainees' desks, but you've got to keep an eye on them – they're sneaky.

Apostrophes will bedevil many writers as long as we have them. Arguments for not having them at all do exist. As for hyphens, they don't have many functions, but one of them appears to me in uncharitable moments to be ensuring an abundant supply of inconsistency. You're unlikely to hear "Stop the presses!" ring out in newsrooms outside old Hollywood films. From where I sit, "Should this have a hyphen?" will be heard every 15 minutes or so.

What follows is a look at our basic bits of punctuation and issues with them. And if it's issues you're after, there's no better place to start than with the apostrophe.

What could go wrong with apostrophe's?

Hunting out apostrophe errors wouldn't be a bad hobby for people slow to anger. Blunders are easy to find, making tracking them untaxing for error spotters low on energy. It's a hobby that can be pursued indoors with minimal equipment: one internet-connected computer and one desk for hitting one's head against should slowness to anger not be as strong a trait as initially thought. In birdwatching, the object of attention knows how to fly away. Misplaced apostrophes just sit there, be it in the virtual world or at the local shops. It wouldn't come as a surprise to learn that obliging greengrocers keep fresh supplies in large boxes at the back of their premises, ready to put them on display as prices rise in times of scarcity and fall in times of plenty, whether for carrot's, apple's, mandarin's or cucumber's.

Apostrophes tell us we have possession, a close association or omitted letters on our hands. The basic rule about apostrophes and plurals is straightforward, although prepare yourself for an exception or two that will soon come into view. (English doesn't go anywhere without its best friends: exceptions.) If all that is being created is a garden-variety plural, do not throw in an apostrophe. It doesn't help; it won't win any prizes. What's more, people will think you've been careless. Is it fair that this mistake is known as a greengrocer's or grocer's apostrophe? No, but their signage practices haven't helped their cause over the years, even if they are far from the only perpetrators. Surely we could pick on the powerful instead. The odd Silicon Valley entrepreneur must have misused an apostrophe at some point. Why not change the name to the tech billionaire's apostrophe?

Seek and ye shall find people who fear proper apostrophe use is dying as quickly as the most trusting of dodos squawked its last squawk, if squawking is what dodos did. Retired British subeditor and self-confessed pedant John Richards achieved global attention after founding the Apostrophe Protection Society in 2001. The organisation supplied pro forma letters that concerned citizens could customise and send to offenders in order to point out with great civility the error of their ways. Richards was awarded a satirical Ig Nobel Prize at Harvard University "for his efforts to protect, promote and defend the grammatical difference between plural and possessive". He was honoured as Mr October in a calendar of Britain's dullest men, where he was in impressive company as it also featured the head of the Roundabout Appreciation Society.

Although he was often ignored and failed to persuade British businesses such as Harrods and Selfridges that they were in desperate need of apostrophe insertion, Richards, who died in 2021 aged 97, did score a victory in 2013 when the Mid Devon District Council reversed a decision to ban apostrophes from street signs. It wasn't enough, however, to keep him from announcing in 2019 that the society's time was over. Fewer people than in the past cared about getting their apostrophes right, he said, and "the ignorance and laziness present in modern times have won!" Despite that sense of defeat, the society lived on under new management.

At the other extreme from the Apostrophe Protection Society are the people who feel nothing would be lost but exasperation should the apostrophe disappear. Don't be surprised if abolitionists break out the champers and start hugging startled strangers should it be no more. The critics argue that English survived without the apostrophe before the 16th century; it's not a punctuation mark that has earned its keep since; and meaning can be worked out from context anyway, which is what we do all the time in speech without fuss. Where critics do allow for ambiguity, the argument is that it's rare. Notable voices are on the list of detractors. Calling the apostrophe merely "moderately useful", Robert Burchfield, editor of the four-volume *Supplement to the Oxford English Dictionary* from 1957 to 1986, wrote in the 1980s that the time to abandon it was near given the level of misuse. Linguist Geoffrey Pullum has said he wouldn't miss it and no harmful confusion would result from its disappearance. There's this from George Bernard Shaw, who apparently knew a vulgar microscopic organism when he saw one:

There is not the faintest reason for persisting in the ugly and silly trick of peppering pages with these uncouth bacilli.

How to herd apostrophes

The fact remains that we haven't dropped apostrophes in standard writing yet. At this point in humanity's journey it would be a shock not to see them in media reports, books, the average business document or an essay.

Contractions

Apostrophes didn't come to us as a way to deal with possession. Blame or credit for them goes to French printer Geoffroy Tory, who introduced them into French in the 16th century to show when something was left out. English printers pounced on the idea and ran with it, leading to our customary apostrophe use to indicate that letters have been omitted. We're all familiar with this sort of thing: *don't, can't, I'm, you'll*. Writers are commonly advised to avoid contractions such as these in formal writing as they'll sound too chatty. It's a matter of deciding what tone you want or need to convey, although total avoidance can sound stilted. I like a good chat, so contractions are sprinkled throughout this book. That's not to say I'm a fan of *should've* and *had've*. Those two in their written form are not pretty, as handy as they are in everyday speech. *Shouldn't've* is out of the question.

Apostrophes can also crop up in cases of numerical omission when the century being talked about is obvious. An actual '80s mullet haircut is to be avoided at all costs, but the apostrophe signalling that 1980s has been given a trim has survived innumerable changes in hairstyle fashion.

Possessives

Denoting possession is a matter of asking ourselves who or what something belongs to, selecting a well-honed apostrophe and then inserting that carefully crafted specimen at the end of the answer to the question. Call on the services of an apostrophe and an *s* for most singular nouns and a lone apostrophe for most plural nouns:

> *the porcupine's parrot* (one porcupine in prickly possession of a feathered companion)
> *the climbers' calluses* (multiple rough-skinned mountaineers in need of hand cream)
> *Sammy's seals* (one Sammy, proud owner of you know what)
> *the boss's biscuits* (one boss who would be better off possessing celery sticks)
> *the princesses' personal assistants* (more than one royal possessed of servants and therefore a cushy life)

Usage guides differ about whether to add an *s* after the apostrophe for singular names ending in *s*, but the more common line of attack is to go by whether that *s* is pronounced:

> *Dickens's dictionary*
> *Jones's jitters*

Ah, but people don't necessarily pronounce such examples the same way. Also blessed with the seal of approval are:

Dickens' dictionary
Jones' jitters

Where two pronunciations are possible, you could pick a version of a name and stick with it, or you could take a streamlined route. Applause broke out in my workplace about a decade ago when we adopted the less common style of using *s'* for all names ending in *s*. No more thinking about pronunciation or fearing discovery of the following in reports written by people who thought they had to use *s's* no matter what (there were some):

Woolworths's white radishes (yuck)
the Seychelles's seashells (additional yuck)

Writers who want to complicate the situation (not recommended) will find usage guides that advocate an apostrophe without a subsequent *s* for biblical and classical figures (*Jesus' birth*, *Moses' beard* and *Socrates' wisdom*) but an *s's* approach for everyone else (*Hawkins's nail clippers*). Sometimes these guides also throw in an exception to the exception: if the classical figure has a single-syllable name, *s's* it is: *Zeus's thunderbolt!*

Plural family names trip up some writers. Two members of the Roberts family are not the Roberts but the Robertses. Here's the done thing when the need arises to go down the possessive route, although the more unwieldy the result the more attractive a solution that moves the apostrophe away from the name becomes:

> *the Harrises' hot water bottles*
> *the Fernandeses' fillings* (Drill down into the Fernandes family's fillings instead.)

At this point I picture some readers jumping out of armchairs, raising their hands and starting to mouth, "But what about ...?" Fair enough. A further complication can be avoided no longer, the one encountered in situations such as these:

> *farmers market or farmers' market*
> *girls school or girls' school*
> *writers festival or writers' festival*

On the one hand, it depends; on the other hand, it still depends. Is there possession going on, or are the words *farmers*, *girls* and *writers* merely doing some noun describing, behaving like adjectives? This can go either way. Pick one and head for the hills with it before anyone starts an argument about heading for the sea instead. If the farmers owned the market, they'd no doubt like to see an apostrophe (*farmers' market*). If only one farmer owned it, a *farmer's market* it would be. If it were thought of as a market *for* farmers, *farmers market* would be fine.

Girls' school/girls school and *boys' school/boys school* are classics of the genre. Should I set up the Black Stump Girls School, legions of people, me among them, would back the absence of an apostrophe. The girls don't literally own the school; it's a school *for* them. However, apostrophe-possessing schools (some of them frighteningly expensive) do exist and have their supporters too. If you head out to dinner with one of those supporters, you could be in for a scintillating evening of discussion about apostrophes not only applying to literal possession but also to a close relationship.

Meanwhile, Australia's literary landscape is blessed with the Sydney Writers' Festival but the Melbourne Writers Festival – yet another sign the two cities will never resolve their differences.

Using a database of 100 million words, a Lancaster University study released in 2021 found that in the 30 years since the early 1990s, apostrophe use in the sorts of examples where things could go either way was down by 8 per cent. If this trend continues, those who named the Melbourne Writers Festival will have reason for smugness. Whether writers like it or not, however, they all must own the state of their skin. An apostrophe is appropriate in *writers' wrinkles*.

The wisest course at this point is to head for firm ground. I know where some can be found:

> *The Los Angeles smog is breathtaking.*
> *A United Nations plumbing emergency is under way.*
> *A Rolling Stones satisfaction shortage has broken out again.*

That which appears before *smog*, *plumbing* and *satisfaction* is working in a descriptive, not a possessive, way. Apostrophes are sometimes wrongly added in such cases. If you're ever not sure, run a test using something that doesn't end in *s* and the difference is clear even if the smog isn't:

> *the New York smog*
> *a worldwide plumbing emergency*
> *a Coldplay satisfaction shortage*

Possessive pronouns don't take apostrophes, leaving us with *theirs*, *yours*, *his*, *hers*, *ours* and the troublemaker *its*. Losing sight of the fact that an *it's* with an apostrophe is the contraction of *it is* or *it has* is as common as cereal for breakfast. If all the people who mix up their *its* and *it's* were to be placed in one room, the room would have to be the size of Canada.

Seekers of simplicity will like this one: official Australian geographical names don't take possessive apostrophes, and so the nation is home to places such as the Fishermans Bend urban renewal area in Melbourne, the Sydney suburb of Badgerys Creek and the town of St Helens in Tasmania. Controversial punctuation aside, it's a policy that promotes uniformity and removes any suggestion an individual owns a chunk of our shared public space. It means there is no need to try to work out what to do about Surfers Paradise. Do the surfers own the paradise, making it Surfers' Paradise, or is it a paradise for surfers and so Surfers Paradise? Or could there be just one lucky surfing god in possession of a veritable Surfer's Paradise? Dispense with the apostrophe on all occasions and tell objectors you're acting in accordance with government policy. They will find that many parts of the cosmos are unnamed should they wish to stake an apostrophe-laden claim a few light years away.

The UK has a mix of pro-apostrophe and anti-apostrophe place names, but the US federal government has been shunning possessive apostrophes in geographic names since the 1890s, tolerating only a handful of exceptions such as Martha's Vineyard. The archives of the US government's Board on Geographic Names offer no explanation for the policy, although the board labels as a myth the theory that it had something to do with apostrophes looking too much like non-existent rocks when printed on maps.

The apostrophe in *children's* goes right there, between the *n* and the *s*, not after the *s*. There is no such word as *childrens*. The Melbourne-based Murdoch Children's Research Institute used to have an apostrophe-deprived *Childrens* in its name but eventually dusted off a suitable candidate and put it where it would be expected to be found. As the institute's focus is medical research and it's at the fore of that sort of thing, I trust apostrophe sticklers were kind to it back in the day.

Having said at the start of this section that apostrophes aren't usually used to form plurals, it's time to let the exceptions loose. We do indeed dot our *i*'s and cross our *t*'s. There's scope for an apostrophe in the *do's* of *do's and don'ts* too, lest our first thought, should it not have one, be to make it rhyme with *boss*.

Elsewhere, this sort of thing takes an apostrophe:

five years' jail
six weeks' notice
two minutes' warning
1957's best headline
one day's wage

This sort of thing doesn't take an apostrophe:

back in the 1950s
two months pregnant

And these are pretty wild but we're used to them:

menswear
womenswear
childrenswear

That last one is going too far for my taste, but I swear all three are in common use without causing riots.

* * *

So whither the apostrophe in the 21st century and beyond? I suspect withering will be a big part of its future. Many people don't know how to wield it or can't be bothered. Others believe it is at best a nuisance that deserves to disappear. In 2021 a London *Times* editorial suggested apostrophe decline wasn't worth getting worked up about. Will it be gone in 30 years? I wouldn't go as far as to predict that. Maybe its use in contractions will fade the most as this century progresses, which strikes me as a little annoying if you want to distinguish *he'll* from *hell* in a hurry, but not the most hellish of fates once context is taken into account. *Didnt*, *shouldnt*, *arent* and *isnt* are clear enough and would not take long to get used to. Perhaps apostrophes will make only occasional guest appearances, hanging around for the odd *he'll* that crops up on a rainy day.

I have no intention of being at the forefront of, or even contributing to, apostrophe decline, but if it continues I'll see it as an understandable drift rather than a disaster. I'll keep using my apostrophes in the way standard English calls for. To abandon them or, worse, to head down the greengrocer route would jar and cause great consternation among too many people as things stand. And, apart from anything else, becoming an apostrophe maverick would not be conducive to subeditorial employment. Dear boss, gee, how I love apostrophes.

Let us pause: commas

Looking for an excuse for an argument? You could head to Texas and get a debate rolling about the US Constitution's Second Amendment, the one about the right to bear arms. Is the individual being given a general right to arm-keeping and to bear the darn things, or is the amendment ratified in 1791 talking specifically about firearms linked to state militias? Avoid bearing arms while the argument rages. The version in the US National Archives says:

A well regulated Militia, being necessary to the security of a free State, the right of the people to keep and bear Arms, shall not be infringed.

That's cleared that up then – or not. Look at the comma placement among those 27 words. It's only added to the debate. What might have been fine in the 1700s, or otherwise, leaves a modern-day reader wondering if what we're faced with is the work of a foundling four-year-old comma scribe rather than an expression of Founding Fatherly intent. By modern standards, the first and third commas are just weird. Legal experts and grammarians have argued over the significance of the commas to that sentence's meaning and will no doubt continue to do so. I'm backing away from resolving American gun issues. My point in raising the puzzling punctuation is merely to stress again that commas matter and comma care is a marvellous thing.

Commas were used more erratically in the past and more frequently. Authors lacking an idea of how to punctuate or just not interested could leave it to printers to guess as to where to deploy a squiggle or two. The gods of chaos had much to smile about. When thought did go into comma placement, it tended to be more about suggesting where you might take a breath than highlighting the grammatical structure of a sentence – more about rhythm than clarifying meaning.

This is at the heart of what complicates commas. We want them to help with our pauses, our rhythm, our tone, but we also want them to help with understanding. It can be a lot to expect from such a tiny creature. The emphasis is on the grammar today, but the dual role still causes confusion and arguments. It's seen with other punctuation too, but commas are where the issue is at its most heightened. We lean towards lighter punctuation in modern times, but some people want more commas and some want fewer still. Others want to head for a spa retreat where any comma that causes a triggering incident is immediately ejected.

Listed entities

Commas do nicely when they help us make lists, replacing *and* or a modest *or*:

> *The spatially challenged builder and decorator working on little Isla's doll's house bought a two-metre-high rabbit statue, a four-metre-long dining table and a 20-kilogram paperweight large enough to crush the whole premises.*

That kind of construction (the sentence, not the doll's house) will keep Aussies happily listing time and again. But there's another comma out there, the one known as the Oxford, serial, series or Harvard comma. As you may have gathered, its name is the subject of as much passion in some circles as the question of whether it should appear as a matter of course or is mostly a nuisance. It's an extra comma in a list of three or more things, one that goes after the second-last item and before *and* or *or*. In the above example, it would go after the word *table*. Here's another example before an *and*:

> *Wilhelmina likes nothing better than commas, full stops, dashes, and perfectly straight hyphens.*

To abstain from using the Oxford, serial, series or Harvard comma is up there with godless savagery in the view of American copy editor Benjamin Dreyer in his book *Dreyer's English: An Utterly Correct Guide to Clarity and Style*. I'm of the view that we Aussies need look to, and I'm going to pick a name here, the Oxford comma only when it removes ambiguity or if a pause is wanted for stylistic effect. We're responsible grown-ups and don't need it to prop us up at all times, but here's an example where it takes care of ambiguity:

The baker loved his two sons, Kim Kardashian and Kylie Minogue.

Should the urge exist to remove the slightest, split-second prospect that the sons might be named Kim Kardashian and Kylie Minogue, an extra comma will do that.

The baker loved his two sons, Kim Kardashian, and Kylie Minogue.

In the next sentence, an extra comma near the end makes it clear that catering services and restaurants are meant to be taken as one sector.

The sectors most affected by the meat ban are agriculture, vegan activism, and catering services and restaurants.

The absence of an Oxford comma, known as such for its traditional links to Oxford University Press, has cost millions of dollars on occasion. Punctilious punctuators point to the Portland, Maine, case of a dairy company locked in an overtime dispute with drivers working for it. A US court ruled that the non-presence of an Oxford squiggle (my word, not the court's) in a piece of state legislation created enough uncertainty to make it appropriate that the drivers' claim for overtime should succeed, leading to a $5 million settlement in 2018 and no doubt merriment in homes inhabited by Oxford comma lovers across the land.

Elsewhere, as we think about commas and lists, use a comma where *and* could be inserted in a string of adjectives:

> *The caring, devoted, ethical tyrant appears that way only in his own dreams.* (The caring and devoted and ethical tyrant appears that way only in his dreams.)

There's no need for commas in something like this:

> *The bright purple shade his face turned as it came to match his new violet jacket suggested further consumption of lollies within the purple range would be unwise.*

Rare is the person who would run around talking about *bright and purple* or *new and violet*, so that's that.

When commas go pair-shaped

Commas are used in pairs to bracket off parts of sentences. This is a good thing, but, as mentioned in Chapter 2 in discussing Goldilocks' fussy eating habits, there's a distinction to be made between bracketing off essential words and non-essential words. If you've got something that provides essential information about a noun that comes before it, something that's defining information, don't add commas separating it from the rest of the sentence. Consider this theft case, the aftermath of which provides a searing commentary on humanity's struggles in an uncaring universe:

A man who stole 20 TV sets doesn't understand why he still can't find anything to watch.

If you place *who stole 20 TV sets* in commas, you're telling readers that the information isn't essential to the logic of the sentence, that it's non-defining, just extra detail thrown in by the by as part of a sentence in which what matters is the following (I beg to differ):

A man doesn't understand why he still can't find anything to watch.

And there is a difference between these two:

Australian builders who erect houses that lack roofs annoy home buyers. (Only those builders who erect roofless houses, the roof-neglecting being defining information, are annoying.)

Australian builders, who erect houses that lack roofs, annoy home buyers. (All Australian builders are annoying and, by the way, they're all roof-neglecting rotters.)

This sort of thing often crops up in the media:

The pest controller, Miriam Wordley-Smuthers, has written a book on keeping termites for fun and profit.

Good for her, but this sentence is telling us she's the only pest controller. If preceding sentences haven't established that only one pest controller is being talked about, get those commas out of there. The world has many pest controllers, and punctuation etiquette calls for that to be acknowledged with a comma-free reference to the pest controller Miriam Wordley-Smuthers.

Strictly speaking, in the next example we appear to have a bigamist on our hands:

Arturo's wife Emma is an inventor of useless gadgets.

This suggests Arturo has more than one wife and the defining information is that the wife being talked about is the one called Emma. Should he not be a bigamist, commas around Emma will show that her name is non-defining, that it's by-the-way information, and the record is set straight.

When commas are meant to appear in pairs, the second one gets forgotten surprisingly often. Should a pair be appropriate within a sentence, that means two, by definition a non-negotiable one plus one:

The house, a mud structure perched on the edge of a crumbling cliff, will be topsoil by morning.

The house may be reduced to topsoil by morning and be no more, but the same should not be said of the comma needed after *cliff*.

Splicing things up

Comma splices make me think of ice cream, I think particularly of a vanilla ice cream with a tangy coating. The Splice ice cream is refreshing after a swim on a hot day, and I say that without financial inducement from its makers. It's rarer to come across a comma splice that has refreshment value. You won't find it coming with financial inducement either. It's what you get when you use a comma to join what can stand as two sentences, as at the start of this paragraph. Here's another one:

> we were all going direct to Heaven, we were all going direct the
> other way ...

Journalists are most likely to start unconsciously splicing when quoting people, as if somewhere between the quote being uttered and its transcription an unwanted stream-of-consciousness vibe entered the room. On the bright side, splices are easy to fix. Replace the comma with a full stop or a semicolon. Or you could throw in a co-ordinating conjunction such as *for*, *and*, *but* or *so*. Words known as subordinating conjunctions – *while*, *although*, *because*, *if*, *since* and their friends – also come in useful for digging a splicing writer out of a hole.

Some style guides rail against the splice; others allow a little leeway. I'm all for keeping it out of conventional news reports, academic writing or business writing, where it looks like the writer didn't know what they were doing. In the hands of fiction writers, at least the ones who happen to know what they're doing, a splice can create a special effect such as a sense of haste, a poetic quality or an air of informality. Many a famous writer has happily spliced. The "we were all going direct to Heaven, we were all going direct the other way ..." splice on the previous page is the work of one Charles Dickens. He chose to keep up his momentum and splice his heart out at the start of *A Tale of Two Cities*:

> *It was the best of times, it was the worst of times, it was the age of wisdom, it was the age of foolishness, it was the epoch of belief, it was the epoch of incredulity, it was the season of Light, it was the season of Darkness, it was the spring of hope, it was the winter of despair, we had everything before us, we had nothing before us, we were all going direct to Heaven, we were all going direct the other way ...*

Could he have kept that up for much longer? Well, he isn't known for his brevity but perhaps not. Should the novice novelist try something similar? Maybe stick to something short. "I came, I saw, I conquered" is an oldie but a goodie in the splicing repertoire.

Just briefly

Let's mull over these guys and whether they need commas:

Last month I found five commas by the side of the road.
On Tuesday I ate five commas for breakfast.
I stood on a comma but it didn't yelp.

In keeping with the modern practice of light punctuation, commas can be skipped when phrases and clauses are brief enough to be digested all at once.

But to stress again the point that well-wielded commas are great ambiguity busters, here's where one would be helpful:

After eating lions tend to watch reruns of The Lion King.
After eating, lions tend to sit around moaning about how unhappy they are with the Cowardly Lion character in The Wizard of Oz.

A longer bit at the start of a sentence makes a pause appropriate:

As every last comma in the fridge had been eaten by her brother, Portia was left to make do with a meal of full stops.

The comma in that sentence also dispenses with the momentary thought that the brother is named Portia, which is a good thing to do in at least 99.9 per cent of mentions of brothers.

CHAPTER 5

MORE THINGS THAT PUNCTUATE OUR LIVES

Hot, bothered and hyphenated

Hyphens hurt, hyphens are perverse, hyphens are maddening. Readers of the earlier section on comma splices will note that I've just felt the need for some splicing even though I have spent much of my professional life as a splice removalist. That's what hyphens will do to you until you settle down, learn to stop looking for consistency and adopt some rules of thumb. Do we, don't we, did we, will we, should we? The answer is yes, no, maybe, sometimes. There are people who spend none of their waking hours thinking about hyphens, and there are those of a more striving nature, people constantly seeking an answer to one of life's great riddles: does a hyphen go here? Hyphens link words and parts of words. It sounds simple and sometimes it is, but don't depend on that.

Many expressions start out as two words. Somewhere along the line a hyphen appears. People like it and get used to it. It spreads. But cometh the day a one-word version bursts onto the scene. The wise hyphen will know that its reign is at risk if this thing takes off. The drift from hyphenated to single word is to be seen everywhere. Even *today*, *tomorrow* and *tonight* were hyphenated until early last century as *to-day*, *to-morrow* and *to-night*, although the thought of a parallel universe with *tod-ay*, *tomorro-w* and *tonig-ht* is somehow appealing. You won't see many *to-day*s today, but other terms have different versions floating about that have equal acceptability: land owner, land-owner, landowner; co-operate, cooperate; nonfiction, non-fiction; home buyer, home-buyer, homebuyer; and on it goes.

It's a popularity contest and may the best version win. The more familiar something becomes in hyphenated form instead of two words and then as one word instead of hyphenated, the faster one-word domination draws near. The drift can also go the other way, from hyphenated back to two words. *Ice cream* is an example, although it is with relief that I report the flavour is unaffected whether a hyphen is an ingredient or not.

It's often the modern way to drop hyphens with common prefixes such as *cyber*, *mega*, *mini*, *over*, *super* and *under*. Thus we're familiar with *cybercrimes*, *megastores*, *miniskirts*, *overjoyed*, *superstorms* and *underwhelmed*. *Co-ordinate* and, as mentioned, *co-operate* go both ways, but I've yet to see a *coowner* and would rather not.

If you want to feel confident you're doing the popular thing, accept that consistency is elusive and get thee to a dictionary. The people behind those are keeping an eye on usage and will settle on an entry accordingly. Tranquillity will be more obtainable if only one dictionary is used. A rival publication will probably take the opposite position and it's best you don't know that.

Confession time: I cheat when I encounter quite a few of the shorter everyday words ending in *-up*, *-off* or *-out*. As there is no consistency to be found with these and they appear so often, I've taken to hyphenating many an *-off* and *-up* word and leaning towards one word for their *-out* cousins: *stand-off, bake-off; check-up, mix-up; turnout, checkout*. I may have no supreme right to do this, but my aesthetic biases lead me in this direction, and it frees up scarce brain space to focus on more important matters. I'm not talking about verb situations. If it's a verb situation you're in, two words are required:

You will stuff up that fruitcake if you add garlic. (verb situation)
This is the biggest stuff-up since the great fruitcake failure of 1923. (noun situation)
This is a stuffed-up fruitcake. (bonus adjectival situation)

The *Oxford* dictionary people hit the headlines in 2007 when the sixth edition of the *Shorter Oxford English Dictionary* ditched 16,000 hyphens, sometimes creating single words, sometimes shifting back to two words. *Fig leaf, test tube* and *water bed* joined the two-word camp; *bumblebee*, *chickpea* and *waterborne* went from hyphenated to one word. The *Oxford* people looked at 2 billion words used in sentences from 2000 onwards in newspapers, books and blogs and on websites to help them decide what to do. The editor of the sixth edition, Angus Stevenson, said at the time that people were not confident about using hyphens any more. He also pointed to book, magazine and newspaper designers finding the humble horizontal line messy and old-fashioned.

Designer disapproval aside, we need hyphens in the multi-word concoctions known as compound adjectives, or at least we do much of the time. A big test is whether ambiguity exists without a hyphen. Writers have a lot of discretion in this area, but good karma will flow to those who spare readers from taking something the wrong way:

> *a man eating eggplant* (unremarkable)
> *a man-eating eggplant* (best avoided should life and limb be important)
> *a little used fly swatter* (could be too small to tackle an outback onslaught)
> *a little-used fly swatter* (could have plenty of surface area and plenty of swats left given lack of use thus far)

In keeping with the modern tendency to keep punctuation to a minimum, compound adjectives made up of words that regularly go together don't need a hyphen. The meaning is clear from the start:

a nursing home resident
a human rights watchdog
a primary school teacher

Compounds using adverbs ending with *-ly* don't need a hyphen. In adverbs we have modifiers of verbs, adjectives or other adverbs. No one presented with the phrase *a sartorially challenged garbologist* would come to the rubbish conclusion that *sartorially* could go with the noun *garbologist* (*a sartorially garbologist*) rather than with the word immediately after the *-ly*, the adjective *challenged*. Think of the *-ly* as doing away all on its own with any ambiguity. Only the churlish would view it as part of a conspiracy to make life harder than it has to be in these cases:

a deeply puzzling attitude to fly-fishing
A badly cooked truffle is no fun, Gus.
Publicans called last drinks on a critically endangered species of orange-bellied bar-hopper.

Could there be a complication about to creep into view? Of course there could. Not all words that end in *-ly* are adverbs. A hyphen is used in the case of non-adverbs:

A curly-natured question has decided to go straight.
A family-oriented cruise will come with at least one spa opportunity for six-year-olds.

Whereas the adverbs mentioned earlier would not work as adjectives with our examples (no *deeply attitudes* or *badly truffles* need apply), *curly* and *family* are capable of doing so: *a curly question, a family cruise*.

What we need now is a straightforward hyphen use that will offend no one. Praise is owed to any higher power out there for the simple way hyphens excel at preventing confusion among *re-* words:

reform and re-form
resent and re-sent
recreate and re-create
resign and re-sign

Usage in numerical situations is straightforward too:

forty-five
a first-rate meal
a six-year-old small person (but *a small person who is six years old*)
a four-year delay
one-third

A word about dashes

Fight any temptation to throw hyphens and dashes about in place of one another indiscriminately, even if the latter look a lot like hyphens, albeit ones that have been stretched on a rack. While hyphens are busy linking words and parts of words, their rack-stretched cousins mostly serve as alternatives to commas or brackets – as in this case – or to semicolons or colons. They can signal an abrupt change of thought. I'm having an abrupt change of thought right now – send in the dash purveyor.

The dashes in the previous paragraph are *en dashes*, which are about the width of a capital N and the ones journalists in Australia and the UK tend to stick to when dashing about. There are other ways en dashes make themselves useful. It's standard in book publishing, for instance, to use them in place of hyphens when a horizontal line is called for with a proper name of two or more words: *a post–Cold War* sale of bargain missiles. As well, they're used with numbers, dates and times to show a range: *a 5–2 victory, March 3–24, 2–4pm*.

You'll also see *em dashes* (—) strutting their stuff from time to time. They're roughly the width of a capital M and are particularly common in American usage, frequently appearing without spaces—in this kind of way—when replacing brackets or commas. Should one character in fiction be interrupted by another, an em dash signals that too. Some authors – Hi, James Joyce – prefer them to quotation marks, using them at the start of lines to signal dialogue, but that's their business. We don't use them at all in my place of gainful employment. If I were going to be mean and insult them, which I am, I'd call them too loud and intrusive.

As celebrities will attest, overexposure can do bad things to a career. If a dash has already appeared on *The Real Housewives of Beverly Hills*, does it really need to turn up on *I'm a Punctuation Mark ... Get Me Out of Here!* in the same week? No. That show already has an apostrophe, an ellipsis and an exclamation mark. It's crowded in the jungle. Some people forget there are commas and colons and are prone to overdoing their dashes. Too much of that sort of thing – as this sentence is about to show – gets dizzying – and that's a fact.

Colonic irritation: the colon and the semi

If the apostrophe is the reigning monarch in the realm of controversial punctuation, the colon is a mere foot soldier guarding the palace. It's harder to get worked up about it. It doesn't crop up as often as the apostrophe. When was the last time you heard of it inspiring the creation of a colon protection society? It has been called old-fashioned and people get it mixed up with the semicolon, but for the most part the colon does a respectable job of saying here comes some information. H.W. Fowler of usage guide fame had a memorable way of putting it, describing the colon as "delivering the goods that have been invoiced in the preceding words". The sentence you're reading now and the next one are each equipped with a colon as they're introducing examples:

> *A dog with a matted coat needs three things: a wash, a telling-off and instruction in the use of a brush.*

Colons can also be used to introduce quotations:

The dog, told to brush its own coat, said: "Woof!"

As with the 1960s TV series, the *Mission: Impossible* film franchise uses a colon in its title. Some posters for *Mission: Impossible III* used two: *M:I:III*. Is that overkill? If subtlety is preferred, pick a different movie.

Semicolons give us a compromise, providing a pause heavier than a comma but with less weight than a full stop. This is appropriate when you consider they consist of a comma with a full stop on top. They have also been known since the 1990s for their tendency to wink wryly ;-) I'm not sure how to add a full stop to the end of that sentence without ruining the aesthetics of my emoticon and so shall leave it at the wink and beg forgiveness. It would be interesting to know how many winks have appeared this century, but the chance that anyone has counted them all is slim. So much of human endeavour goes unrecorded.

SPOT THE DOG   SEMICOLON THE DOG

Representations of eye movements aside, many millions of us will go through life without using a semicolon, a piece of punctuation considered to have been brought to us via Italian printer and publisher Aldus Pius Manutius in the 15th century. He was a busy man, having also pioneered italic type and introduced the closest thing to paperbacks in those days. As with the colon, production volume of the semicolon is much smaller than that of commas, full stops and apostrophes. In Greek, it takes the place of our question mark. Among its English-using detractors it has a reputation of being pompous, unnecessary and old-fashioned. George Orwell decided it was superfluous and chose to avoid it in his novel *Coming Up for Air*. I like to use it sparingly and am happy it exists. It's useful when joining independent clauses (ones that can stand as separate sentences) that share a closely related thought, creating a juxtaposition or counterbalance.

The children brushed the dog's coat; the dog refused to assist. The dog demanded walkies after his coat was brushed; the children demanded payment.

You could use a full stop instead in those cases, or a dash, or a comma followed by a *but*. It's a matter of rhythm and whether you're in the camp of the semi-lovers, the semi-neutral or the semi-haters. Stay away from the camp of the semi-deranged, a clique founded on the misapprehension that the semicolon is a mere plaything that adds oomph in place of any old comma.

Getting back to legitimate uses, semicolons in certain types of lists remove ambiguity where items within a list need a comma for their own purposes:

The dog's plan for walkies included heading for the gum tree across the street for light relief; catching up with the poodle next door, the cavoodle two houses down and the groodle that haunts the park; and messing up his coat again to annoy his beloved humans.

???? and !!!!

We're pretty good as a sophisticated society at including question marks at the end of questions. The practice is not endangered. However, we do sometimes show confusion as to what qualifies as a question when words such as *perhaps*, *maybe* and even *wonder* are on the scene. The examples below are statements, although witnesses have spotted similar sentences appearing with question marks. In speech, some people make such sentences come across as questions by pronouncing them with a rising intonation at the end. Adding a question mark if you really must in informal writing or dialogue is one thing, but it's not a strategy that has yet gained a place in formal writing, where full stops prevail:

Perhaps a question mark at the end of this sentence would be disastrous.

Maybe I'll deploy a full stop.
I wonder if question marks ever get bored when faced with all that questioning.

Rhetorical questions are questions asked for effect and without expectation of an answer. They're a way of making a point. Some sources say a question mark is always needed regardless; others allow for using a full stop or an exclamation mark. I like the latter view, which is well established and considers the sense of what's being said:

You've spilled your drink over me yet again, haven't you. Have you gone mad!
Your behaviour is atrocious, may I just say.

It's standard procedure to frame instructions and polite requests as questions but drop the question mark. A boss speaking to an employee or a parent to a child is undoubtedly issuing an order in the next two instances, so there's a strong argument for a full stop:

Would you get your foot off my desk.
Will you stop hitting your brother with that banana.

I'd use a question mark with the next instance, which is a request that comes with a fair amount of doubt:

Would you grab me a Mercedes-Benz while you're at the shops?

We've now arrived at the never shy exclamation mark! This one has a lot of nicknames depending on what part of the world you're from, among them the shriek, the bang and the screamer. Hollywood columnist and author Sheilah Graham said F. Scott Fitzgerald's advice to her was to cut out all exclamation marks as using them was like laughing at your own joke.

Social media users and texters of the *!!!!* school of written communication would dispute that. In these circles, a single exclamation mark is considered as flat as a full stop, and serious exclaiming can only be done if punctuation moves in packs. In a rough-and-ready poll on Twitter a few years ago asking how many exclamation marks were needed to convey genuine enthusiasm, three was the winner, receiving almost 35 per cent of the 798 votes.

Careful authors in more formal settings keep their exclamation marks to a minimum and use one at a time. Just as *!!!!* has yet to become an accepted part of formal writing, *!!* remains edgy too. Using that sort of thing in a report of a scientific study will not end well:

We put the chemical into the test tube and then we put the test tube in the test tube holder!!

Restrained use has its place. "The blowfly buzzed off with my can of Mortein!" wouldn't have the same sense of urgency or shock without a little exclaiming. Exclamation marks can also inject warmth or other emotions into an otherwise sterile email: "Thanks!" Tabloids love them; more serious news outlets impose strict rationing.

Don't overquote me

Have you noticed this "sort of thing" when reading news sites? Journalists spend so much time quoting other people that we can get into the habit of overdoing it, putting quotation marks around the most ordinary of words someone has uttered. The practice is rife even though all this quoting should be saved for unusual, disputed or significant remarks:

> *The professional organiser said he "just adored beyond all words" a well-placed coat hanger he saw yesterday.* (yes to quotation marks)
> *The organiser says coat hangers are "useful".* (quotation mark annihilation called for)

Installing quotation marks around a word or phrase to inject doubt, irony or sarcasm is fine: "The 'grand feast' consisted of toast and a cup of tea." The extra punctuation distances the writer from the quoted words. What's not wanted is what many a sign gets up to, its writer having held the mistaken belief that quotation marks add

an impressive bit of emphasis. Ask the internet to show you *scare quotes*. Frightening examples such as the following will appear:

Fireworks "you can trust"
Beware of "dog"
"No" happy hour
Please enjoy our "safe" and "comfortable" flight

Back in the realm of appropriate quotation mark use, some people prefer single inverted commas, while others go down the double route, shunning the belief that less is more in these matters. I'm in the latter group after decades of over-familiarity with newspapers, where the double approach is common. Australian books, however, tend to be single-minded (though I won the argument in this one). Whichever path you choose, be consistent, which is a great way to look like you meant it.

A colon or a comma can be used to introduce a quotation. Meanwhile, the most common practice in Australian and British English when a final comma or a full stop is reached is to place it inside the quotation marks when a complete sentence is quoted:

The punctuator said: "Here I am, happily quoting with my double quotation marks."

Whether you use single or double marks, do the opposite for a quotation within a quotation:

"My teacher told me my violin playing sounded like 'dozens of car alarms going berserk at once', but I refused to stop," the student said.

If a partial sentence is quoted, a comma or full stop will happily sit outside it:

The teacher told the student he'd heard better playing when a startled cat jumped on a "broken-stringed, clapped-out excuse for a violin".

If your quoted material runs over more than one paragraph, save the closing quote mark for the end of the quote, but repeat the opening marks at the start of each paragraph.

The student said: "He told me I could make a living by recording my violin efforts for use in car alarms.
"I was horrified and ran from the room screaming."

Brackets aren't only for squares

Does one want Kardashian-like curves ( ) or the straight up and down of Kate Moss [ ] when it comes to brackets? And does it matter if Kim has subjected her curves to a squish with the help of an item from her shapewear collection? What Kim does with her curves need not concern us, but bracket choice does make a difference. These fellows [ ] are used to make it clear that words inserted into a quote come from the writer of the overall piece rather than the speaker or the author of the quote:

"I know I left [the invisibility cloak] somewhere, but now it's just not showing up."
"I tried holding up my bookshelves with [curved brackets], but now I've gone full circle and it's still not working."

Aim to keep your square-bracketing to a minimum. Too much makes a quote hard to read, meaning you would have been better off paraphrasing it in the first place. Use round brackets, sparingly, if the words they set off are from you:

These are my round brackets (found down the back of the couch).

The wonder of dots

There's not a lot to say about full stops. Use of them at the end of sentences is still looked upon favourably. They are common but not compulsory at the end of abbreviations that aren't strings of initials and that don't finish with the last letter of the word: *Tas.* for *Tasmania* but *Dr* for *Doctor Strange.* However, it's the height of fashion, darling, to dispense with them in initialisms such as these: the *ABC*, not the *A.B.C.*, and *NSW*, not *N.S.W.*

Three dots in a row can be used for trailing-off purposes, such as when you nod off before you reach the end of writing a ... The three dots form an *ellipsis*, a device that pops up within sentences and between them to show that something has been left out. Is there ever cause for four dots to take into account a spot where a full stop would normally be? There are people who have given this topic much thought and have provided fiddly and contradictory answers. I'm not one of them. I stick with three dots and avoid getting into a frenzied debate with myself or anyone else. In a startling example of dot proliferation, as many as six dots can be found in the Chinese version of the ellipsis. China's a huge country, one where much is done in a big way. If it wants six dots, six dots it shall have.

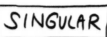

CHAPTER 6

THINGS THAT LIE
IN WAIT TO TRAP US

How nice it would be if global leaders had nothing more to concern themselves with than language hazards. We could send them off to summits where they could work to ensure that international supplies of subordinate clauses were plentiful, non-polluting and showing no signs of insubordination. Presidents and prime ministers could hold urgent talks on the sidelines to try to reach agreement between nouns and verbs while the rest of us got on with daily living. Sad as it is to say, our leaders are busy with other issues, and grammar pitfalls cannot be left to them. It's up to us to avoid getting into traps and to get ourselves out of the ones that have already ensnared us. What follows is a look at a few common traps, ones that even English-speaking global leaders fall into despite their best efforts to leave grammar to flunkies.

Modifiers that go rogue

Misbehaving modifiers are everywhere. If newspapers and online news sites were ever to go a day without any, that should be a major news story, at least on a slow news day when every politician in the land stayed silent, everything operated efficiently and no one was annoyed about anything anywhere. If the news story on the absence of misbehaving modifiers (more properly known as misplaced modifiers) managed to be free of them, that in itself would be noteworthy.

This kind of stylistic problem arises when a word or longer part of a sentence is separated in an inappropriate way from whatever it's meant to modify or describe. The result is jarring. The intended meaning will usually be grasped, but not always. If you don't have to, why cause even a moment's confusion, unintended mirth or the mental equivalent of a groan? Society has enough of those. Let people get their fill elsewhere.

One type of modifier that delights in tripping us up is called the dangling modifier. It's trying to modify a part of a sentence that's missing or in the wrong spot, and the words left dangling are usually at the start of a sentence. They're meant to be doing description duty about someone or something, but that someone or something has gone astray:

Preparing to leap tall buildings, the Superman costume was donned.

"Preparing to leap tall buildings" is a modifier, but the only subject it has to modify is "the Superman costume". The person preparing for the leaping is missing when he's the true subject. He needs to get dressed and hurry into the sentence. He also needs to abandon delusions about his leaping skills if he cares about his safety. We can't help him there, but we can adjust the sentence in various ways:

Preparing to leap tall buildings, Arthur donned the Superman costume.
Arthur donned the Superman costume in preparation for his display of high-rise leaping.

I have a real-world dangling modifier that I've kept in a cage for several years. If offered crumbs and a little water, it sometimes promises to behave, but you'll see what the problem is. The name has been changed to protect the guilty, including any newspaper subeditors who were lurking in the shadows when it slipped past:

A favourite gift for friends and family, Martina likes to fill pretty old plates with shortbread.

Given that she has favourite-gift status, do relatives leave Martina under the Christmas tree every December and then banish her to the back of cupboards where the tea cosies knitted by Great Aunt Gertrude are kept? Yes, readers can work out what's really going on.

But they're busy, and the requirement to do mental gymnastics may send them away to raid a packet of shortbread rather than continue with an article about turning it into gifts. We wouldn't want the shortbread on those plates to be stale and dust-covered by the time family members work out whether they're getting Martina or the baked goods for their special occasion. Solutions exist:

> *A favourite gift for friends and family, pretty old plates filled with shortbread have long given Martina an excuse not to have to think of more expensive presents.*

The next real-world example, one from a court case, also comes with adjustment to protect the guilty. A stylish cat is along for the ride too:

> *Dressed in a suit and wearing dark glasses, Portman's cat could be seen wandering past as he asked for his matter to be adjourned.*

Danglers aren't going to disappear. Some flow past harmlessly. Considering the overall situation, the need to hunt down the worst of the ambiguity monsters should take priority. The sentence before this one contains a dangler. It doesn't explicitly say who is doing the considering, but the answer is not in doubt.

Danglers have relatives: squinting modifiers (squinters to their friends) and other modifiers in the wrong spot. Squinters create ambiguity because they can be read as modifying material to their left or right. Many words come to mind when thinking about how to characterise them. There's one description starting with *use-* but it doesn't end in *-ful*. Here's a squinter:

Cycling up hills rapidly hardens one's resolve to stay out of the Tour de France.

Is it only furious pedalling that makes that resolve rock solid, or is it any climbing attempt? Shifting the *rapidly* to before or after *cycling* would solve the problem should furious pedalling be to blame. A shift to after *hardens* would make clear that the hardening is rapid.

Elsewhere, modifier groans roll on with these sorts of misguided examples capable of creating the wrong image:

The picnicker chased an emu in high heels after it stole her biscuit from the table. (The picknicker was wearing high heels as she chased the emu that stole her biscuit.)
Go and ask that man in the dark jeans called Alfonse. (Ask that man called Alfonse. He's the one in dark jeans.)
We served chicken wings to the guests wrapped in cling film. (We served chicken wings wrapped in cling film to the guests.)

Bottom line: modifiers and people wielding them need to know their place.

Tautology

So often, if it's worth saying once, it really is worth saying only once. I've been resisting *safe havens* for ages on the grounds that if a *haven* isn't safe it isn't worthy of the name. The *safe* is redundant. Dictionaries confirm a *haven* is a safe place, but I know that whenever I see mention of one these days, it will come with a *safe* leading the way. I expect I'll keep resisting for now, but I do so with a sense of futility. If enough English users like their havens to come with added safety, then *safe haven* will be just another conventional phrase to add to the collection. In principle, avoiding tautology makes for writing that looks more thoughtful and prevents wasted words. Some things, however, take on a life of their own and become set phrases. *PIN number* is an entrenched example. We say it, we write it, we don't think about it, even though *PIN* stands for personal identification number.

96

If, though, you'd like to join me in the tautology resistance movement, here are a few others to get to work on. Removing words that serve no purpose is a noble endeavour, and a good place to start is with a tautology search and destroy mission. I've chosen examples where the chances of success are better than in those dangerous places where havens and PINs are to be found:

pre-order in advance (Don't we need to pre-think about that?)
warn in advance (No, after the lion attacks will do.)
5am in the morning
new innovations
past experience (In a timey-wimey manipulation of the space-time continuum, the Tardis-travelling Doctor brought to us by the BBC can have future experience. As for the rest of us ...)
armed gunman (Has he got a knife as well?)
died of fatal wounds (Let's call this doubly tragic.)
consecutive days in a row
give birth to two twins
major disaster
over-exaggerate
free gift
first discovered (It's no to this unless something's been discovered, forgotten about and rediscovered.)
proceed forward (Consider this the only way to go.)
revert back (see above)

close proximity (They don't make a far version.)
true facts (These have been judged to be the best kind.)
necessary requirement (We really don't need this.)

In skilful hands repetition can be a stylistic choice that adds emphasis and focuses the reader, unlike the offenders above. Edgar Allan Poe used the device in his poem *Annabel Lee*, which has the following lines that don't call for tampering with:

And so, all the night-tide, I lie down by the side
Of my darling—my darling—my life and my bride,
In her sepulchre there by the sea—
In her tomb by the sounding sea.

A tautological *tomb* follows that *sepulchre*, but to Poe's credit there's not a *safe haven* in sight.

Subject–verb slugfests

Verbs and what they go with need to match – most of the time. It's called subject–verb agreement. Is the subject singular or plural and how does that affect the verb? We're lucky that we don't have to bother any brain cells with the word *you*. Whether talking about one person or 10, the verb *are* does a sterling job of accompanying it. In other cases, we pick up well before anyone tells us in school that our subjects and our verbs should be agreeably aligned:

I am going to
we are going to
it runs
we run

As with young siblings promising to behave for the whole day, however, the subject–verb agreement principle is prone to wobbles in practice. A common wobble among speeding journalists, not that we are the only perpetrators, occurs when something starts out being treated as a singular but then makes a switch:

The company has declared a small profit for the year but are confident of turning in a whopper next year.
The Coalition is split over climate change but are meeting on Thursday with the aim of producing a warmer atmosphere.

It's as if by the time the latter part of a sentence has been reached the first part has been forgotten. The impression that a long coffee break has been taken between segments does arise. After I typed that, my spelling and grammar checker alerted me that I'd initially written *impression ... do arise*. I have mixed feelings about this, being appreciative of its vigilance and disturbed that it's another sign the technology intends to throw a hissy fit, elbow us humans out of the way and do it all itself.

Meanwhile, back to the wobbles and one of those slip-ups that happens when you start talking about *one of those*. Strictly speaking, I just slipped up. The *happens* that appeared in the first sentence of this paragraph should have been *happen*. Despite the prominent appearance of *one*, the *happen* relates to the plural *slip-ups*. Turning the sentence around shows the relationship:

> *Of the slip-ups that happen in discussion of wobbles, this is one.*

Some pundits are of the view singular or plural can apply in this kind of situation. I would think most people would take a singular route and not notice. I'm persisting with the plural, at the very least as a sign of occasional sympathy for sticklers.

What's to be made of that *one* word in phrases such as *one in five*? Should it be *one in five people is* or *people are*? You could stick to the straight and narrow and opt for an *is* to stay in agreement with the *one*, but there's a decent argument that *one in (insert favourite number here)* isn't really talking about one person or thing, despite the presence of, well, a *one*. *One in 10 Sydneysiders* is talking about 10 per cent of Sydneysiders, or more than 500,000 people. Each approach has its supporters and I can see merit either way. Pick one of them and run with it. It could become your grammatical equivalent of a signature scent. There's young Mei going down a plural route again. So fragrant.

In *either/or, neither/nor* sentences, a singular stance is usual, but if the noun or pronoun closest to the verb is plural, adjust the verb accordingly:

Either the author or the editor has drunkenly overridden the spellchecker. Did you see how ljfrmkl *was misspelt as* jlrfklm*? Neither the spellchecker nor the writers have a clue as to how skyscraper was "corrected" to* ghbvtsd.

Measurements, periods of time, sums of money, etc generally fall into the category of single ladies, as Beyoncé might have sung but didn't. The chance is still there for her to consider working the following kind of thing into her lyrics. In each case the subject at hand, even if no lady, is treated as a single unit:

Two kilometres down the road is too near town to conduct nuclear testing.
Three years is no time at all in a cell when prison officers forget to lock the door.
Fifty dollars isn't going to buy so much as a cup holder, no matter how much you beg your local Maserati dealer for a discount on a showroom vehicle.

Next up, it's fish and chip time. Two nouns joined by *and* would usually take a plural verb, but English won't let us off the hook that easily. When words go together as closely as *fish* goes with *chips*, they can be treated as a single entity:

Fish and chips is the bread and butter of our business.
Bread and butter is served with the fish and chips.

Should you wish, things that aren't always wedded to one another may also be treated as single units depending on the sense of the sentence:

Suffering and annoyance is/are inevitable if the chip shop has run out of batter. Rage and frustration is/are bound to follow.

There is, or the contracted *there's*, is a common sentence starter in everyday speech no matter how many things follow it. In writing, *there are* expectations that *are* will be used with more than one thing:

There is no need for any is *issue.*
There are an is *issue, an* are *conundrum and a* there *puzzle arguing over in the corner.*

Collective upsets

Collective nouns – words such as *audience, team, group, couple* and *family* – are regular causes of head scratching as to whether they should be treated as singular or plural. They may be talking about a single entity, but that entity contains more than one person or thing. Either option can be valid depending on the sense of the sentence. The trick is to avoid sounding unnatural as a result of taking too rigid a stance. Is it the entity as a whole that's being brought to mind or its individual parts?

His audience raised their eyebrows as the fraudster insisted he
had a smartwatch for sale that had been worn by Rembrandt.
The gang of fraudsters were running in every direction as police
came upon the smartwatch stash.
The family were coming to blows over who got the Rembrandt
smartwatch Dad just paid $50,000 for.

In these cases, the images created are of individuals with eyebrows, individuals running around, and individuals fighting, so treating the collective noun as a plural sits best. In the next examples the opposite applies:

The committee is ready to announce the results of its smart-
watch fraud investigation.
The government is monitoring the situation.

Having taken a deep breath, I now feel able to broach the touchy subject of sporting teams. I say touchy because my Melbourne colleagues who specialise in sport never quite recovered after the decision was taken to switch our default style to plural for these to bring it into line with what our Sydney colleagues were doing. British English often adopts a plural policy in talking about teams: Manchester United *are* winning. Leeds United *are* not winning. It's a convention found in Australia too. I can't say anything further about Manchester United or any other sporting team united or otherwise without highlighting my sporting illiteracy and disappointment that the sports section did not take up my suggestion that tiddlywinks was worthy of prominent coverage.

COLLECTIVE CLOWNS

By the way, if you ever want proof of the creative potential of English, look up a list of collective nouns for birds, animals and people. Most of the entries won't be seen beyond lists of these things, but you will get a sense that they were dreamt up with all the enthusiasm of Toad in *The Wind in the Willows* yelling "Poop, poop!" while hurtling down the road in a new-fangled motor car. Along with the more familiar *gaggle* of geese and *pod* of whales, it's possible to talk of an *exaltation* of larks, a *pandemonium* of parrots, a *murmuration* of starlings, a *shrewdness* of apes and a *flamboyance* of flamingos. *A skulk of foxes* sounds like a good name for a band. Ravens have been lumbered with an *unkindness* or a *conspiracy*. It could have been worse, as shown by a *murder* of crows.

Many such terms date back to the Middle Ages. Chloe Rhodes, in her book *An Unkindness of Ravens*, points out that they served as a way to distinguish the aristocracy, who were taught them, from the masses. Amusement played a role too. Surely, the creator of a *drunkship* of cobblers was smirking at the time.

A whom? Ahem

Learners of English should be cautious about approaching native speakers in the street for advice about avoiding the *who/whom* trap. It's a trap people tend to think of when the word *grammar* comes to mind, but the chance of a street encounter ending in anything other than bewilderment and deeper brow wrinkles (Botox users excepted) is slight. Native speakers will know there's a difference between the two. Beyond that, many of them will be as puzzled about *whom* as learners and wish their urgent trip to stock up on the latest grammar books hadn't been interrupted.

Whom's social standing is not what it used to be, as the advice from one senior journalist to a colleague to just stick a *who* everywhere and be done with it attests. Outside a few well-known phrases, its appearance in conversation is rare. Opting for "To whom did you give the extra chicken nuggets?" over "Who'd ya give the nuggets to?" isn't the done thing. *Whom* lives on in formal writing – for now – but even when it crops up there, it's at risk of appearing where a *who* belongs. Some uncertain writers wanting to sound impressive, or taking an "if in doubt throw in something that sounds classy" approach, overdo their *whom*s.

A painless method for working out what goes where does exist. If substituting *he*, *she*, *I* or *they* works, you're in *who* territory.

These are the words used when talking about the subject of a sentence, the doer of the action. If it's *him*, *her*, *me* or *them* you end up with, you're in *whom* land, the place the object, the receiver of the action, calls home:

The man who stole the Mona Lisa *thought the Louvre was giving it away as it had been left on its own hanging on a wall.* (*He* stole the *Mona Lisa,* so *who* it is.)

The accomplice with whom Michelangelo plotted the crime was his daughter. (Michelangelo plotted the crime with *her,* so *whom* it is.)

This is who ruined my day with a who/whom *question.* (*She* ruined your day, so get out your *who.*)

To whom it may concern: stop ruining my day. (It concerns *her.*)

The next instance is an example of a situation where people go astray by overdoing their efforts to look sophisticated. It's the grammatical equivalent of wearing evening attire to an event where the dress code is smart casual:

Mel is a serial offender whom I think will never learn the difference between evening attire and smart casual. (Pretend *I think* isn't there: Mel is a serial offender *who* will never learn.)

The basic *who/whom* trick also helps with *whoever* and *whomever*:

Whoever likes blue cheese needs a taste bud readjustment.
(*She* likes blue cheese, not *her* likes blue cheese, *so whoever* is
what we're after, even if blue cheese is not what we're after.)

I gave the blue cheese to whomever I could get to take it.
(I got *them* to take the blue cheese by insisting I'd pay for
its disposal.)

It's not hard to imagine a time when *whom* catches up with our
dearly departed dodos in the extinction stakes. Few will miss
it. Even so, it would be taking historical revisionism too far to
remove it from well-known examples. We should resist any urge
to tinker with the John Donne line from *No Man Is an Island*
about never sending to know "for whom the bell tolls". The poet
knew a decent spot for a *whom* when he saw one back in the
17th century. It does add solemnity in that case, don't you think?
And Ernest Hemingway knew what he was doing when he chose
that phrase for the title of his novel published in 1940.

CHAPTER 7

THE THING ABOUT AMERICAN ENGLISH

Ah, Americanisms. Raging against language habits created by people in the Land of the Free who feel it's "the land of the free to go our own way with English" is fun up to a point. But who let that air of defeat into the room and why is it settling in for a long stay? I was once amused by an excitable British newspaper style guide that tended to thunder "Abomination!" at any whiff of American infiltration. It's been a standard subject for style guides of the non-American persuasion to get upset about, and for readers to complain about.

We're understandably wary of cultural domination from afar and attached to home-grown language contributions. A sense of loss and nostalgia is natural when looking back at pithy local idioms that have died away. But we can't live in a bubble. English has made an art form of borrowing from just about any other language that happens to stroll by on a sunny day in the park. It can't help borrowing from versions of itself as well. Purity is not its forte. Many of us might not like the lopsidedness of our cultural exchange with the United States, but the exchange itself has been inevitable.

This isn't an argument for indiscriminate Americanism-hurling. Fling that out the door right now. If something jars because it hasn't settled into the Australian way of operating or doesn't fill a need for a new word or phrase, I'll be flinging it you know where. We don't have to be overly sensitive to be irritated at this point in our language development should a fine *footpath* become a *sidewalk* or a family in Perth run out of *gas* while heading to the *drugstore* in a *pick-up truck* to buy *diapers*, having just *deplaned* after a Bali *vacay*. It's safe to say that in making his "all the way with LBJ" remark at the White House in 1966, Australia's prime minister at the time, Harold Holt, was not talking about Lyndon Baines Johnson's way with words. No siree, Bob.

Yet for all the fears that Australian English is under threat from Americanisms, in 2021 the director of the Australian National University's National Dictionary Centre, Associate Professor Amanda Laugesen, described it as thriving. She said in the State Library of NSW's *openbook* magazine that loss was natural in any language but thousands of potential new local entries existed for *The Australian National Dictionary*. When you think about it, *cobber* and *strewth* aren't what they once were, but *seachangers*, *democracy sausages*, *barbecue stoppers*, *utes*, *mozzies* and *ambos* are going strong. Take heart.

Will *sidewalks*, *diapers* and *drugstores* be irritating to Australians in 100 years should the US retain its cultural power? Maybe we've reached peak Americanism and our own diverse society will keep us well stocked with pithy ways of expressing ourselves, including further contributions from Indigenous languages and other cultures. Or maybe the *diapers* are coming. In the meantime, hey, *hey* has now become common in place of *hello* or *hi* among many Australians, not that *hi* took off without the help of Americans either. It's been a long time since we were irritated by *OK*, or *okay*, if we ever were. The prevailing explanation for that is that it came from the US, and it's not as if we're going to hand it back. Bill Bryson in his book *Mother Tongue* looks upon it as arguably America's greatest gift to international communication. It's short, to the point and ubiquitous. It even has at least one book to call its own: Allan Metcalf's *OK: The Improbable Story of America's Greatest Word*.

Other "gifts" that we've become used to include *lengthy*, *snag* (as a verb – fear not, the sausages are safe as *snag* for sausage is thought to be of British origin), *teenager*, *discombobulate*, *pantyhose* and *program* over *programme*. We're happy to drive around in *trucks* rather than *lorries*; we only infrequently baulk at talk of *elevators* over *lifts*; and we'll watch American *movies* or British *films* without a second thought, even the 12 instalments in superhero franchises that weren't up to much the first time around. Many of us are content to say we live in *apartments*.

In the 1980s, Stephen Murray-Smith wrote a book called *Right Words: A Guide to English Usage in Australia*. His Americanism list included *I'll call you* (as opposed to *ring* or *telephone*) and *veterans* (as opposed to *returned servicemen*). The cultural cookie did not crumble his preferred way. It's hard to imagine anyone complaining about those today. The federal government won't be, or at least not the Department of Veterans' Affairs.

As mentioned earlier, however, there's a difference between organic language change and recklessly embracing before bedtime every Americanism that pops its head up in this part of the world. The following remain high on my list of peeves. If you can't instantly work out which column is waving the flag for Australia and which is American English, ban yourself from US streaming content for a month and see if that helps:

bangs	*fringe*
burglarizing	*burgling*
candy	*lollies*
parking lot	*car park*
downtown	*CBD, city centre*
flashlight	*torch*
garbage can	*bin says it all in seven fewer letters*
gas	*petrol (OK, our version is longer.)*
math	*maths*
restroom	*toilet*
sweats	*my kingdom for trackie dacks*
transportation	*transport (unless it's the convict-era variety)*
trucker	*truckie*
upscale	*upmarket*

Condemning Americanisms is a sport in some quarters, and one that goes way back. It's pre-pre-pre internet. *Notes on the State of Virginia* by Thomas Jefferson, a Founding Father, the principal author of the Declaration of Independence and the third US president, was published in London in 1787. In it he used *belittle*, which he may have been fond of as he's believed to have coined it. That *belittle* ruined the day, possibly the remaining days on this earth, of at least one anonymous British critic, who wrote:

> *Freely, good sir, will we forgive all your attacks, impotent as they are illiberal, upon our national character; but for the future, spare – O spare, we beseech you, our mother-tongue!*

H.L. Mencken, an American journalist and author, wrote about the language divide in his 1919 book *The American Language*. By 1808, he noted, the journal *The British Critic* had "admitted somewhat despairingly that the damage was already done – that 'the common speech of the United States has departed very considerably from the standard adopted in England.'" In the same year, another journal, the *Annual*, had "pronounced its high curse and anathema upon 'that torrent of barbarous phraseology' which was pouring across the Atlantic, and which threatened 'to destroy the purity of the English language.'"

Should precision punctuation placement be one of your hobbies, you may have noticed the partial quotations at the end of each of the preceding two sentences come with full stops inside the quotation marks. That's American English for you. It even happens if the partial quotation is only one "word." In Australian and British English, the full stop is much more likely to go outside the quotation marks in these cases. I'll refrain from calling the American preference an abomination but feel compelled to say it leaves the rest of the sentence looking like its full stop has been (Americanism alert) burglarized.

Language changes for all sorts of reasons and at differing paces, but some Americans worked hard to help the process along. Teacher, lexicographer and writer Noah Webster, who in 1789 argued that "a future separation of the American tongue from the English" was "necessary and unavoidable", was famously successful or an infamous perpetrator of abominations, depending on your point of view. He's the Webster of *Merriam-Webster* dictionary fame. He gained a reputation for being unlikeable and a humourless snob, but his *American Spelling Book*, first published in 1783, sold tens of millions of copies, more than 100 million by some accounts.

Neither Britain nor the Antipodes would have been begging Webster to do book tours, but his mission to remove silent letters and standardise the language made the US Defense Department, Pearl Harbor and the Centers for Disease Control and Prevention the possessors of American-style spellings they are today. It's common in the Australian media landscape to change these to *Defence*, *Harbour* and *Centres* to reduce reader irritation. Some people may find it presumptuous to change proper names, but as I have seen Sydney Harbour rendered *u*-less in *The New York Times* on occasion and Britain's National Theatre referred to as the National Theater, all's fair in love and international journalistic practice.

Webster's *silent k* extermination success in words such as *publick* and *pathetick* was mirrored elsewhere, as was his preference for *jail* over *gaol*. We're not fellow travellers with *traveled*, but we shouldn't forget that some of what we think of as American could be found long ago in British English anyway, including that *center* spelling and *-or* endings. Webster had his flops too: no spellchecker or autocorrector wanting to keep its job would accept his suggested *masheen* over *machine* or *tung* over *tongue*.

Language flows in more than one direction, even if the Americans are winning and Australia has a lot of catching up to do. In one positive development, the hugely successful cartoon series *Bluey*, produced in Brisbane and about a blue heeler pup and her family, has been doing a fine job of introducing Australianisms to impressionable American children – and their susceptible parents. For instance, the word *dunny* has reportedly been heard coming out of young American mouths. Bluey cemented her cultural status in the US by appearing in the 2022 Macy's Thanksgiving Day Parade in New York, so there's hope for further language infiltration yet.

Leaving aside young Bluey's success, I tried an internet search for Australian words used by Americans but came up with only lists of our words Americans don't understand. Hand me some straws to clutch at and I'll conclude Americans are at least aware of *g'day* and can work out what it means. They're also aware of our unique fauna. Of particular cultural significance is the kangaroo. Without our appealing marsupials, the American children's television show *Captain Kangaroo*, a morning fixture for three decades from 1955, might have been cursed with a name like *Captain Hog-nosed Skunk* or *Captain Prairie Rattlesnake*. The link to kangaroos was tenuous (the host used to wear a jacket with pouch-like pockets), but let's not split hairs, not while we're clutching at straws.

Whatever happens next in our lingo exchange with the US, we can take comfort in the fact that the "Great Australian Adjective" has stuck by us through all sorts of language upheaval. That's another way of saying *bloody*, which although not a word Australians came up with, have sole claim to or would let loose in formal writing, was adopted by the nation with unparalleled fervour. The "Where the bloody hell are you?" tourism campaign of the noughties caused consternation overseas, but it undeniably said "Australian". Scottish writer Alexander Marjoribanks noted the extent of the Australian fervour for *bloody* back in his 1847 book,

Travels in New South Wales, and as a dutiful subeditor I have checked that his maths is correct:

> *One man will tell you that he married a bloody young wife, another, a bloody old one; and a bushranger will call out, "Stop, or I'll blow your bloody brains out." I had once the curiosity to count the number of times that a bullock driver used this word in the course of a quarter of an hour and found that he did so twenty-five times. I gave him eight hours in the day to sleep, and six to be silent, thus leaving ten hours for conversation. I supposed that he had commenced at twenty and continued till seventy years of age … and found that in the course of that time he must have produced this disgusting word no less than 18,200,000 times.*

CHAPTER 8

BEFUDDLING THINGS

*"When I use a word, it means just what I choose it to mean –
neither more nor less."*
An imperious Humpty Dumpty sets Alice straight in Lewis Carroll's
Through the Looking-Glass, *having just defined glory as a
"nice knock-down argument"*

On the one hand, there's left; on the other, there's right. Doors often come with two instructions: on one side, pull, and on the other, push. When I'm tired, or wide awake, or anything in between, I get these mixed up. My misguided efforts to override satnavs have forced taxi and Uber drivers into rapid course changes. Until the truth dawns, I wonder why doors I'm trying to push open will not budge. For some, these things are as simple as breathing. For the rest of us, respect for satellite navigation and the invention of automatic doors is advisable. The problem isn't opposites attracting but opposites distracting.

At least these words do not look or sound alike. English gives us plenty that do, and writers of any skill level can end up *practicing* their *practise* or *licencing* their *licenses*. Despite spellcheckers, grammar checkers, autocorrection software and occasional satnav assistance, words go wrong and people like me still have a job trying to remedy the situation when not adding to the confusion. I've perpetrated a few mix-ups beyond *left* and *right* and *push* and *pull* but live in hope that the correction tally provides redemption. May you find your favourite sources of bewilderment among the following examples. The explanations are based on current usage. If Humpty Dumpty has his way, the meanings will all change next week.

adopted/adoptive

People who are *adopted* have *adoptive* parents. *Adopted* pets have pet humans.

affect/effect

Affect and *effect* are common sources of muddlement, and the muddled deserve a simple path to clarity. That simple path involves remembering that *affect* as a verb is an action word. *Action* and *affect* both happen to start with *a*. Done! *A* for action equals *affect*. Those *a*'s were made to be lumped together, leaving *effect* to do noun duty and deal with the outcome:

The bleak weather affected the child's mood, but it had no effect on biscuit consumption as an unsympathetic parent had moved the packet out of reach.

As proof the world can be cruel, *effect* is sometimes a verb (meaning to bring about) and *affect* is sometimes a noun, one used mainly in the context of psychology.

all right / alright

If *all right* has a reputation as a fine upstanding citizen, *alright* is the shady newcomer, around for only a century and a half or so. They're both in use today, but *all right* is the traditional one, the one that gets to wear Chanel while *alright* shops at Kmart. As we already have *already* and *altogether*, it's hard to see the problem with *alright*, but the best way to avoid annoying people is to stick with *all right*. You could encounter a hitch distinguishing between exam results that are *all right*, i.e. all correct, and those that are merely *all right*, as in so-so. If they're your results, just tell everyone you mean the former. And before anyone raises it, I'll get in first and say the rise of *alright* is not an argument for accepting *alwrong*.

alternate / alternative

Would you like to live in an *alternate* universe or an *alternative* universe? If the former, you're already in one, the *alternate* universe of American English, where *alternate* is frequently used in places Australian English would call for *alternative*. In Australian and British English, *alternate* is a verb meaning to take place by turns repeatedly. It's also an adjective with the meaning of every other. An *alternative* is a choice or another possibility:

> *Alternative routes to success for the well-groomed psychopath include lying, cheating and stealing.*
> *The well-groomed psychopath and his like-minded partner alternated in annoying the rest of humanity on alternate days.*

As mentioned earlier, I'm not one for roaring "Abomination!" at the sight of the slightest Americanism. However, I am yet to get used to *alternate* universes, even if I can see a time when they win the argument. In 2017 Kellyanne Conway, an adviser to Donald Trump, described falsehoods about the size of the crowd at his presidential inauguration as "alternative facts". No, they were just falsehoods, but it was kind of her to use *alternative*.

altogether/all together

Alright may struggle for recognition alongside *all right*, but *altogether* has made a name for itself by performing a service not offered by *all together*. While *all together* is busy telling us that people or things are hanging out together, *altogether* is promoting the cause of its own like-minded friends *wholly*, *totally* and *completely*:

He was altogether pleased to find his house had remained standing after the wolf next door had huffed and puffed in an attempt to blow it down.

The jigsaw pieces were all together until little Samantha decided to deprive her brother of one by putting it in a safe deposit box in Switzerland.

amuse/bemuse

Bemuse belongs with words such as *confuse*, *puzzle* and *baffle*, all of which are appropriate considering how easy it is to be under the impression it means the same as *amuse*. We have *amusement* parks rather than *bemusement* parks, although the British artist Banksy and his collaborators did their best to change that with the dystopian theme park Dismaland, which popped up in England for a month or so in 2015. The staff were trained to be surly and to wish visitors a dismal day. Cinderella's pumpkin coach crashed and the Dismaland castle was a wreck. That's *bemusement* for you.

annex/annexe

Annex without an *e* on the end is what's wanted for the verb, as in a country taking possession of territory without being polite and asking first:

Dictatoria wants to annex half of Defencelessia.

Annexe with an *e* is a noun, say an additional building or the awning attached to your family's caravan. You may remember the latter from long summer holidays as a child when the extra living space an *annexe* provided enabled you to get away from your annoying younger sibling. If you were the annoying younger sibling, it meant you couldn't be quite as annoying as you would have liked. An addition to a document such as a report may also be an *annexe* with an *e*. *Annex* as the noun appears in Australian English, but I'm attached to the distinction.

bacteria/bacterium

Word has it the lonely *bacterium* was shunned by all the other *bacteria* after their host watched the movie *Mean Girls*.

biennial/biannual

This book's opening pages came with a suggestion to avoid *biennial* and *biannual* because people who can remember the difference are a rare breed. Seek help if you're experiencing any urge to use one of them. The *bi-* bit is easy, a convenient clue that there's a vibe in the room involving the number two. You may feel confident about tossing in the odd *-ennial* or *-annual*, but the person on the receiving end could come away with the wrong meaning or no meaning at all. Usage charts show drops in popularity for both of these words since the 1950s.

For the record, *biennial* refers to once every two years or something continuing for two years and *biannual* to twice a year. *Semiannual* can be used in place of *biannual*. Those truly determined to be on top of these matters could remember *biennial* by thinking of those big exhibitions with arty themes held around the world every two years. The rest of us shouldn't torment ourselves with the thought that English was devised by a sadist nonchalantly pulling out a baby seal's whiskers while sprawled on a chesterfield. The sofa wasn't a chesterfield for a start.

bimonthly/biweekly

We're not out of the *bi-* woods yet. Does *bimonthly* mean every second month or twice a month? Dictionary definitions say it means both, which surely qualifies it for a prize at the biennial Great Waste of Space Awards. The same problem applies to *biweekly*. Ways around the issue exist. Tell people you exercise fortnightly, twice weekly or every two months and they'll actually have an idea of what you mean. Use *bimonthly* or *biweekly* only if the aim is to obscure an inadequate exercise regime.

can/may

Can I just say, it's a rare soul who doesn't use *can* in the sense of asking permission. Five-year-olds are no longer likely to face a mini-lecture on the *can/may* distinction should their choice of words when pleading for a piece of chocolate be "Can I, can I, can I, pleeeaase?" before descending into "Gimme now!" However, the distinction does crop up in formal writing. If you want to sound formal and especially polite, saving *may* for seeking permission and *can* for talking about ability to do something will do the trick as long as you don't add an insult at the end of the sentence.

canvas/canvass

One *s* for the fabric and two for soliciting votes, proposing something for discussion or seeking someone's opinion whether it's boring or scintillating.

capital/capitol

The United States *Capitol* Building was stormed by protesters on January 6, 2021. The 26 *capital* letters of the English alphabet were not what had enraged them.

STORMING THE CAPITAL

change / reform

Discernment is a good thing, and so is *reform*. A lack of discernment in using the word *reform* isn't a good thing. Politicians can be found in the wild calling any policy change they have in mind a *reform*. The R-word then flows through into the media jungle and out to civilisation beyond, even though one person's *reform* may be another person's *disaster*. We can agree that a policy shift helping to safeguard the Amazon rainforest is a *reform*. Let's leave in the *change*, nay *disaster*, category a scheme to send in politicians once a month to talk to the trees about the benefits of deforestation.

chord / cord

It's *cord* for the rope or string. We have vocal *cords*. Music has *chords*, groups of notes. Something strikes a *chord*. Noting that *cord* has links to the Latin *chorda* (catgut) and *chord* to the Middle English *cord* (short for *accord*) would only create frustration. I just did. I'm sorry, but sometimes the truth must be faced.

compare to / compare with

I like to think that if Bill Shakespeare had had a stereotypical ocker rellie, Bruce the Bard would have been the singlet-attired Antipodean's name. Imagine young Bruce having written a sonnet that began:

Shall I compare thee to a rippa, you beaut summer's day?

If he had, would he have been trying to liken his beloved to the exalted status of cold tinnies, barbies by the pool and hose fights? Or was he setting himself up for a squiz at similarities and differences?

Thou art just as full of hot air but less like a blowfly.

Romantic stuff. There's a subtle although oft-ignored difference between *compare to* and *compare with*. To use the former is to liken something to something else. *Compare with* is used for noting similarities and differences. Should I write that Bruce's work has been compared *to* Bill's, I'm saying it's been deemed to be up there with the Shakespearean canon. Should I write that it's been compared *with*, I'm saying it has been weighed up against that of Bruce's illustrious ancestor. In all likelihood it was found greatly wanting:

Shall I compare thee with Shakespeare?
Thou art more crude and more akin to excruciating.

compare/compere

As TV hosts the world over know, the distinction between *compare* and the hosting duties of a *compere* thrives to this day.

complement/compliment

Both of these hark back to the Latin word *complēre*, meaning to complete. *Complement* has lingered in that neck of the woods while *compliment* has ambled off in the direction of praise. Also, if it's free goods or services you're being given, they're *complimentary*. Remember to *compliment* the person giving them to you.

comprise/compose

A way to happiness with these two is to avoid plonking an *of* after *comprise*.

> *The media tycoon's property portfolio comprises five sheep stations, a Point Piper mansion and a termite mound in outback Queensland.*

The whole (the portfolio) is followed by the parts that make it up. Purists frown on *is comprised of*, the argument being *composed of* or *consists of* is acceptable but *comprise* already has an *of* in its definition: to be composed of. *Comprised of* is common, however, and has been around for centuries. It's hard to see it picking up its *of* and refusing to make any more appearances, but avoiding *comprised of* makes sense if you feel strongly about it or worry about others who may.

council/counsel

A *council* fighting to shut down a ratepayer's backyard nuclear waste disposal operation would be wise to seek legal *counsel*. Should two or more barristers work on the case, the plural remains *counsel*. Psychological *counselling* would be available should the case prove traumatic.

curb/kerb

curb: what one is advised to do to one's appetite in the presence of cake.
kerb: that which causes one to trip when transitioning from road to footpath.

currently/presently

Currently is easy, but *presently* comes with a catch. Appearances to the contrary, it can mean soon as well as at present. Houston, we have a contradiction that no amount of increase in NASA's budget will resolve. Although *presently* started out 500 years ago meaning, no surprise here, at present, it evolved in British English to mean soon. This is the sort of development that Homer Simpson has a word for: Doh! The evolution is centuries old too, so the opportunity to round up the perpetrators is no more. Striking a blow for sanity, American English clung to the *at present* meaning. What has happened, however, is that what became the

American usage wheedled its way back into British and Australian usage. The good news is that the context of a sentence is likely to make the time being talked about clear, meaning *currently* and *presently* have no need to be there in the first place. Upon spotting a *presently* in circumstances where something does need to be said about timing, change it to *currently*, *now* or *soon*, once what's what and when's when have been worked out.

dependant/dependent

It's *dependent* for the adjective and *dependant* for the noun. A person who is *dependent* on someone is a *dependant*. American English reduces confusion by typically using *dependent* for the lot. As this is an Australian book and universal *-ent* usage hasn't won out yet, the advice is to keep a couple of *-ants* in your back pocket for emergency use. You're likely to need a larger supply of *-ents*.

diffuse/defuse

If making an unexploded bomb safe, in which case put this book down now, you'll be needing to *defuse* it. The word comes to us from World War II. It applies when easing all sorts of tense situations. *Diffuse* is about spreading out or being unconcentrated, hence essential oil *diffusers*. Amazon and eBay have aromatherapy *defusers* for sale. Listings often use both spellings, as if the sellers do not trust the customer to get it right and be able to find their product without extra help. On principle, I will not be buying the ultrasonic aroma *defuser* or even the seven-colour bedroom *defuser* until they clean up their spelling act.

dilemma / problem

Whereas a *problem* is any old difficulty in need of resolution, a *dilemma* comes with the extra meaning of a tough choice between equally unappealing options, hence the phrase "on the horns of a *dilemma*". If your only choice in life is to sit on a bull's left horn or its right horn, the message should be clear that climbing on its head in the first place was not a good idea. For purists, there can only ever be two options in a *dilemma*, typical bull anatomy being what it is and the *di-* being an indicator of two, but allowance for more than two is widely made. It's also common to see the word used for difficult situations where no alternative exists. The risk of causing offence with that sort of usage, however, is at least as high as the risk of suffering injury when sitting on a bull's horn. Why court unnecessary danger?

disassemble / dissemble

Disassemble is the innocent one here, meaning to take apart. *Dissemble*'s about hiding or disguising true feelings or beliefs.

disassociate/dissociate

Dissociate will do fine when separation is on the agenda, particularly in psychological contexts, where various dissociative disorders have been identified. *Disassociate* has the same meaning but isn't used in psychology. It also takes two more letters to say the same thing. This isn't a hanging offence but could leave efficiency experts feeling disconnected from it.

discreet/discrete

Discreet means careful or unobtrusive and *discrete* means separate and distinct. The way I remember which is which is that the end of *discrete* looks a little like the end of *separate*, which is handy given its meaning. This tip is of no use to anyone inclined to spell *separate* as *separeet*, but anyone doing that may be beyond help anyway.

emigrant/immigrant

Emigrants leave a country, and *immigrants* enter one. If in doubt, someone devised a simple solution: *migrants*.

enormity/enormousness

This is a big one. Over in the red corner is the view that *enormity* should be reserved for immensely evil acts, monstrous matters (the *enormity* of the crime) and *enormousness* for big things in general (the *enormousness* of the apple tart). In the blue corner we have comfortable users of *enormity* in the latter sense, not least because it's less of a tongue-twister than *enormousness*. Some usage guides accept this; others keep up the fight for the separate meanings. Where I work, we've long accepted the view from the blue corner, perhaps because of how widespread it is or because previous editors of our style guide were practical souls allergic to tongue-twisters. The issue can be avoided with judicious use of *huge* in reference to apple tarts. *Humongous* would be going too far.

espresso/expresso

Sip slowly, and as the caffeine hit takes effect, express not the slightest doubt about this: *espresso* is the spelling that will win you universal approval. *Expresso* froths up to the surface from time to time, but *espresso* is the word we borrowed from the Italians in the first place.

everyday/every day

Advertising signs suffering from the lack of a single space are everywhere. That space makes the difference between *everyday* and *every day*. Beware signs that offer "fresh [insert product] everyday". The one-word *everyday* is an adjective telling us something is ordinary, typical or seen or used each day. If stock is being renewed daily, it's being renewed *every day*. A source with reason to keep an eye on such things has reported that misuse of *everyday* is an ailment to which those in the "wellness" community are susceptible. The day when the popularity of influencers in this area is at least 70 per cent based on spelling ability cannot come too soon. Elsewhere, the song *I Wish It Could Be Christmas Everyday*, recorded by the glam rock band Wizzard in the 1970s, has kept cropping up in the UK charts over the decades despite the egregious, bah humbug-inducing aspect of its title.

famous/infamous

Note that none of the following were called *Infame*: the 1980 movie *Fame*; its hit theme song, *Fame*; the TV series *Fame*; or the 2009 movie remake *Fame*. I raise this because of the surprising number of times I've seen a person referred to as *infamous* when what was meant was *famous*. *Fame* is the desired one of the pair, at least until the paparazzi get too annoying. People strive for it, and it doesn't cast aspersions on someone's character. The same can't be said for *infamous* and its cousin *infamy*. *Infamous* is the sort of word no one wants to be associated with, the sort that can lead to a defamation suit. It shares something in common with *fame* in that it refers to being well known, but it's all about being well known for bad reasons. Well-known war criminals are *infamous*; a social media star who fluffs dance moves on

TikTok is still only *famous* regardless of the trauma caused to viewers. Arguments that as *inflammable* and *flammable* have an identical meaning, the same principle should apply to other words that start with *f* and *inf* don't help. Languages don't work that way.

Not wanting to do *infame* a disservice, I will point out that it is a word, albeit an archaic one. It reached peak popularity in the 18th century, when it was a way of saying to defame or make infamous. Its fame was fleeting. To avoid looking behind the times, stay away from it.

fewer/less

There's a straightforward way of looking at these two. Then, as per standard English operating procedure, there are the exceptions and the arguments. As for the straightforward, use *less* when talking about something that isn't countable:

> *Less time on TikTok equals more time for Instagram.*
> *Less interest in owls leaves more time for admiring kookaburras.*

If referring to something countable, use *fewer*:

> *Fewer people ride unicycles these days.*
> *Fewer aliens consider Earth worth a stopover on interplanetary package tours than did a billion years ago.*

Exception alert! When talking about measurements or money, *less* is fine. It's the overall quantity that matters, not each individual chunk:

> *In less than three weeks, he has learnt how to juggle knives and reattach severed digits. Meanwhile, his influencer sister has reduced her weight to less than 65 kilograms by deploying one simple trick – removing her false eyelashes.*

Should your *less* or *fewer* come with percentages, there are two options. *Less* is usable for the lot:

> *Visiting aliens have met up for coffee with less than 10 per cent of* Star Wars *fans.*
> *Less than 2 per cent of spending by visiting aliens goes towards coffee.*

Or the *fewer* distinction can be maintained for countable things:

> *Fewer than 10 per cent of alien coffee drinkers have been to a Starbucks.*

It is, however, usual to talk about *one less*, making it *one less* problem to solve and *one less* thing to bother about, even though they are countable. Why? Just because. It's standard practice and *one fewer* has paid the price, being left to sound unnatural.

The whole *fewer/less* distinction sounds like a classic of the "just because" genre. After all, we don't fuss about using *more* whether things are countable or not (more oranges, more homework). The distinction is thought to stem from the musings of 18th-century critic Robert Baker:

> *This Word [less] is most commonly used in speaking of a Number; where I should think Fewer would do better. No fewer than a Hundred appears to me not only more elegant than No less than a Hundred, but more strictly proper.*

It's not much of an argument, is it? Passing fancy is closer to the mark. Yet given the passion that still exists in *fewer/less* rows, and widespread recommendations that the distinction be followed, it's not a "rule" I'd recommend ignoring – yet.

Supermarkets have been the focus of *fewer/less* feuds because of their liking for express lanes catering to shoppers with *10 items or less*. The rise of self-checkout areas created a calmer environment as the need for express lanes declined. Tension did break out in aisle eight as pandemic panic-buying of toilet paper became a trend, leaving shelves with *less* toilet paper but *fewer* toilet rolls. In the earlier, more innocent days of the *10 items or less* feuds, some supermarkets kept the peace with a switch to *fewer*. But *less* had its defenders, people willing to see it as a well-established usage that sounded natural or a reference to the 10 items as a whole as opposed to individual items. I go to supermarkets for groceries, not grammar disputes. As long as the items I want are available and reasonably priced, I'm not arguing.

fjord

There's nothing confusing about *fjord*. It's here to provide a moment's pause with nice mental scenery thrown in. This may be needed after *fewer* and *less*. You can render *fjord* as *fiord* if you like, although most people are *j* inclined.

flaunt/flout

If you've got it and you're *flaunting* it, you're showing off or trying to sell something on social media, even if it's only the perfection of your pout. If you're *flouting* the law, you're ignoring the rules and showing contempt. If you're *flaunting* yourself on a social media platform that does not allow pouting, you're once again *flouting* the rules. *Flaunt* is often used in the sense of *flout* but this use has a long way to go to reach the stage where it's well mannered enough to be introduced to parents. *Flout* is only rarely used in place of *flaunt*. "If you've got it, flout it," should never be uttered in front of anyone's parents.

forebear/forbear

These two are troublemakers, the kind that would delight in sneaking up when you've bent down to tie your shoelaces and pushing you over. A *forebear* is an ancestor and *to forbear* is to hold yourself back from doing something, such as impolitely laughing out loud at someone's unfortunate use of *forebear*. Think of the *fore* as matching the final four letters of *before* and you're set for a lifetime of consistent use.

forego/forgo

The sight of a *forego* when talking about going before and a *forgo* when doing without is pleasing. *Foregone* conclusions, the ones asserting that a result is certain, have been precision engineered to start with a *fore-*. Engineers like certainty, and it wouldn't pay to upset them.

foreword/forward

It's that *fore-* thing again – *foreword* for the introductory words at the start of a book, particularly if they're written by someone other than the author of the tome in question. *Going forward* is an unfortunate piece of business-speak, but *forward* otherwise deserves to be looked upon with fondness.

full/fulsome

A safe and simple strategy: avoid *fulsome*. It has a negative meaning but also crops up used in a positive sense in place of *full*. *Fulsome* praise, at least since the 19th century, has been praise that's over the top, reeking of insincere flattery or obsequiousness. That's the standard definition, the one I'm sticking to. However, *fulsome* started out with the earlier meaning of full and abundant and that made a comeback in the 20th century, to the extent that some dictionaries include it. That way problems arise. A *fulsome* flavour won't be mistaken for an insincere one, but thank someone for their *fulsome* praise and stand back in case offence is taken. The *Collins Dictionary* says *fulsome* and *praise* are common bedfellows in journalism and best avoided elsewhere, which reeks of giving up on journalists. However, we're used to being on the outside looking in. Only minimal offence taken.

grisly/grizzly

Lashings of horror and disgust are to be found when *grisly* puts in an appearance. As there are no scary bears putting in appearances in my neck of the woods, I feel no horror or disgust towards *grizzly* bears, only slight unsettlement that they are a type of brown bear with a name related to the colour grey. Brown bears can have fur ranging from cream to almost black, which suggests a name change is in order. Grizzlies often come with grey tips, adding distinction and a little nomenclature logic given that *grizzled* refers to being flecked with grey. Grey-sprinkled beards are *grizzled*. In other *grizzly* uses, *grizzling* children can be silenced by giving them whatever they want.

hang/hung

It's paintings that are *hung* and people who are *hanged*, a strange distinction style-guide writers like to make. The condemned get the comfort of a last meal and the knowledge they will not be mistaken for a Monet masterpiece. What more could they want apart from, ooh, I don't know, a stay of execution? The distinction is worth observing when in the company of style-guide writers, but non-observance when they duck out of the room is unlikely to be remarked upon.

hangar/hanger

That plane taking you on your holiday is sometimes kept in a *hangar*. A coat *hanger* onboard a plane was put to excellent use in 1995 when a doctor on a flight from Hong Kong to London used it along with a knife and fork sterilised in five-star brandy as a makeshift surgical instrument. It was needed during a successful emergency operation on a woman with a collapsed lung. Try doing that with a hangar.

historic/historical

These are often used interchangeably, but there's a helpful difference and it hasn't died out yet. *Historic* applies to things that are momentous and *historical* to anything that's of the past. It could, for instance, be a *historical* fact that a gentleman somewhere got up at 6.32am on August 20, 1771, scratched himself and had a pint of ale for breakfast before picking alarming numbers of nits out of his hair. *Historic* events these are not, at least not to us – no offence intended to any nits who continue to commemorate the Great Nit Massacre of 1771.

The next question that arises with *historic* and *historical* is whether to deploy *an* or *a* before them. That *h* at the start can sound on the quiet side, but it is there. Modern usage leans towards *a*, according to Google's Ngram viewer, which plots what words used in books have been up to over time. *An* was winning until about the late 1930s. People used to say *an hotel* too, but we know what happened to that habit.

hoard/horde

The tourist *hordes* have the privilege of descending on Venice while the rest of us can only watch on as we *hoard* biscuits in times of scarcity.

home in/hone in

Any homing pigeon worthy of its feathery flying licence is capable of moving towards the right destination, *homing in* on it. Should it stick its beak in a pencil sharpener and jiggle it about, it will be doing a spot of beak *honing*. To *hone* is to make something sharper or, figuratively speaking, to improve or perfect it. But (I know, there's always a *but*) *hone in* is also commonly used in the sense of *home in* and getting more common. Think of all those missiles *honing in* on their targets. Sticking to *homing in* will win you more fans, or you could always avoid the issue by *zeroing in*.

I/me

Leaving these guys out of a usage guide would be like producing Tim Tams without a chocolate coating – just not right. It's not

that we go about daily life fretting about whether we should be proclaiming *It is me* or *It is I*. But half a dozen underemployed brain cells want the answer and want it now. Or perhaps they were told long ago but get excited at the thought of repetition. *It is I* is the highly formal choice. It's so old-fashioned that anyone intending to use it might as well be wearing a powdered wig and writing with a quill pen. Join the rest of us in the 21st century and use: "It's me. Open the darn door. I've lost my key."

Here comes the confusion monster again: in the battle between *between you and I* and *between you and me*, *me* is traditionally the grammatical winner – something to do with the objective pronoun (*me*) needing to come after the preposition (*between*), I do believe. You might like to stick to this in formal writing, but daily life is full of *between you and I*'s. The *I*'s emerged long ago, perhaps starting with people drilled in the ways of *It is I*. Shakespeare was an *I* man in the following line from *The Merchant of Venice*:

> *Sweet Bassanio ... all debts are cleared between you and I if I might but see you at my death.*

To work out whether you want *you and I* or *you and me* in *between*-free circumstances, decide if the phrase is the subject of the sentence (the doer of the action) or the object (the person or thing the action happens to):

You and I are going to love this film.
The film annoyed you and me more than fake Tim Tams
devoid of chocolate.

If that doesn't resolve the issue, pretend the other person isn't there:

I am going to love this film.
The film annoyed me more than fake Tim Tams.

Do not seek guidance from the name of the Australian band You Am I. That way madness lies.

imply/infer

"What are you inferring?" is a question heard often, one used to ask what someone is suggesting. Make it *implying*, though, and your approval rating will rise. No one will object if *imply* is used to mean suggest and *infer* is used to mean deduce. They're ways of talking about the same subject from different angles, those of the giver of the information and the receiver:

In saying that potatoes made him sneeze, Mr Smith implied he
didn't like potato chips. I inferred from his comments that
he was the black sheep of the Smith's Crisps family.

The use of *infer* to mean *imply* makes an appearance in some dictionaries, although usage guides tend to frown upon it. I restrict my *inferring* to deducing.

intensive/intents

The common phrase is "to all intents and purposes", not "all intensive purposes". It often pops into my head as "to all in tents and porpoises" but that's because I'd love to make that somehow work as a headline one day. Given that the opportunity to edit a story about a seaside campground visited by porpoises rarely arises, the dream is forlorn.

iterate/reiterate

As with *flammable* and *inflammable* and *habitable* and *inhabitable*, these are the same thing. A waste, you might say, but there you go. There is no point applying logic and refusing to use *reiterate*. You'll only sound odd if you tell people you want to *iterate* a key point.

lay/lie

If there is a god of English, he/she/they/it must have had a chuckle at our expense the day *lay*, *lie* and their variants were dreamt up around a celestial conference table. Once the untruthful version of *lie* is out of the way, we're left with a jumble that has caused grief for hundreds of years.

To lie is to assume a horizontal position; *to lay* is to put something down.

I've burnt my sandwich to a crisp and need to lie down.
To lay a plugged-in charred sandwich press in water is to risk
becoming the human equivalent of burnt toast.

Eric Clapton and Bob Dylan have sold millions of records. Two of those records have added to global *lay/lie* confusion – approach with caution. Strictly speaking, Clapton and his co-writers took language liberties with the song *Lay Down Sally*, unless they meant to ask someone to plonk Sally down as opposed to suggesting to her that she neatly arrange herself. If you're going to be snooty about it, Dylan's *Lay Lady Lay* would become *Lie Lady Lie* (it might get some commas too). Dylan's accolades include a Nobel Prize in Literature. I imagine that comes with the right to defy language convention and *lie* an egg in the name of literary experimentation should recipients so wish.

Lay/lie confusion is understandable when you consider *lay* is also the past tense of *lie*:

I lay down and mourned my late sandwich.

Everyone needs a party trick, and impressing friends with your ability to tell the difference between *lain* and *laid* is surely one of the better ones. Running through the full range of options will show where these two fit in:

I lay the sandwich to rest.
I am laying the sandwich to rest.
I laid the sandwich to rest.
I have laid the sandwich to rest.

If we are talking about lying down, an appropriate subject if ever there was one right now, we get:

I lie down. (Hallelujah!)
I am lying down.
I lay down last Thursday.
I have lain down.

lead/led

It would be nice if the past tense of *read* were *red*. It isn't, resulting in frequent appearances of *lead* rather than the correct *led* as the past tense of the verb *to lead*. The situation is *misleading* and we're easily *misled*.

lend/loan

Friends, colleagues, countrypersons, lend me your ears; I come to bury a language row, not to praise it.

You'll notice Shakespeare's funeral oration for Julius Caesar (even with unauthorised tinkering) involves *lending* aural organs, not *loaning* them. Using *lend* as a verb and *loan* as a noun will keep everyone content, even after all these centuries. It's what I mostly do, but *loan* as a verb has long been around too, especially in contexts such as banks *loaning* us money. If *loan* as a verb takes your fancy, restrict its use to literal *loaning*, that in which something really is temporarily handed over. A stranger offering to *loan* a hand with removal of a credit card from a bag should be viewed with suspicion not only because of fears for card safety. Never *loan* ears, hands or other body parts, although you may figuratively *lend* them.

licence/license

Because of uncertainty or typing fingers racing ahead of the brain, these two can be spotted time and again where they have no business. The United States solved the problem long ago by adopting *license* as the noun and the verb. That caused a problem for the rest of us used to seeing the *-ense* in American writing as a noun and inclined to forget we possess our very own *licence* for that purpose.

lightening/lightning

Lightning may only strike once, but skin-*lightening* creams are common pharmacy-shelf hoggers in many parts of the world and likely to be spotted at close range many times. This information is not provided to encourage use of skin-lightening creams, only to encourage appropriate spelling.

loath/loathe

In *loathe* we have a verb full of great dislike and disgust and in *loath* an adjective with reluctance on its mind. I am *loath* to admit this, but I *loathe* certain English spellings.

loose/lose

Loose lips sink ships. *Lose* your ship and that's a sign you're having a bad day.

noise/noisome

Something *noisome* wafting in from your neighbours' house? Earplugs won't help. To be *noisome* is to be particularly annoying to noses, to be stinky, offensive, noxious, not nice at all. The word is related to *annoy*. A writer calling someone a *noisome* rodent carcass (similar has been said) is not suggesting that person is as loud as a fire alarm going off two metres away.

obsolete/obsolescent

Anything in the first category is outdated and disused; anything in the second is heading that way. Products that are *obsolescent* will be *obsolete* any minute now. It's a plot against credit cards to ensure they regularly leave the safety of their wallets and are used to buy shiny new products.

onto/on to

Matilda may choose to leap with gusto *onto* (to a position on, on top of) the plywood table, but she'll have to *move on to* the task of calling an ambulance after the table collapses. The ambulance will drive *onto* her driveway and the ambulance officers will eventually cotton *on to* the fact she's broken her wrist. Should you wish, using *on to* at all times is a cunning way to avoid any one word/two word issues.

ordinance/ordnance

Once upon a time, *ordnance* struck me as a misspelling of *ordinance*. Then the truth became clear and brain space was reserved for remembering that it's the stuff no one wants to be struck by: the military's weapons, ammunition, fighting vehicles and other supplies. The supplies aren't always of the exciting variety. Presumably someone has to think about soldiers' boot laces too. To suffer a boot-lace malfunction on the battlefield could be stressful. And while battles are being prepared for with all that *ordnance*, local councils will still be producing their rules and regulations, their municipal *ordinances*.

palate/palette/pallet/pellet

If it's the roof of your mouth your tongue is looking for, your *palate* awaits you. If your taste buds are sensitive souls, you have a sophisticated *palate*. A bottle of wine you bought last week may have a rich and oatmealy *palate* with a hint of toasty complexity. Artists wield *palettes*, and colour-scheme co-ordinators may choose from muted or bold *palettes*. A forklift will take you far if a *pallet* loaded with heavy merchandise is in need of moving. Do not try to feed chickens *pallets*; it's *pellets* they're after.

pedal/peddle

Pedalling is what feet get up to when making bikes move and *peddling* is what people trying to sell their wares or ideas get up to. Peddlers on bikes *pedal* and *peddle* with varying degrees of success.

per cent/percentage point

A subeditor of my acquaintance used to interrupt his keyboard clacking from time to time to exclaim, "A journalist did the maths!" Despite the presence of fine number-crunchers in our ranks, he was aware that some of his colleagues were just that teensy bit more comfortable with words than figures and required of him extra attention. As *per cent* and *percentage point* fall into the word category, let's clear up one thing: they're not the same. Let's say *Dancing with the Big Brother and Love Island Rejects* goes from a 10 per cent share of the audience to a 5 per cent share. This is not a *5 per cent* drop. Call it a recipe for cancellation or a victory for good taste, but it can't be called a *5 per cent* drop. It is, however, a *5 percentage point* drop (the simple difference between 10 points and 5 points). What it also happens to be is a *50 per cent* drop. Assuming the overall audience pool has stayed the same, the number of eyeballs watching has halved.

Similarly, if a tax on indecision, a great way to solve government deficit problems, rises from 10 per cent to 20 per cent, it has gone up by *10 percentage points*, not by *10 per cent*. As it has doubled, it has gone up *100 per cent*.

persecute / prosecute

An innocent *prosecutor* going about his everyday prosecutorial business was once referred to as a *persecutor* in a court report I had the pleasure of working on, which is why I raise these similar words here. If the report had been written by the accused, I could understand the mix-up, but ...

practice / practise

We're back in a *licence/license*-like situation. Whereas the US ended licensing confusion for its citizens by adopting the *-ise* ending for either of the L-words, it went the other way with *practice* and *practise*, making the *-ice* ending the more common spelling for both. Adopting one or the other for all four words would have been the user-friendly thing to do, but it was not to be.

Meanwhile, we diligent Australian word-wielders are left to bounce about with the *-ise* ending for the verb *practise* and the *-ice* for the noun *practice*, making it our *practice* to *practise* regularly.

premier / premiere

The *premiere* of *Gone with the Wind* was held in December 1939 at Loew's Grand Theatre in Peachtree Street, Atlanta, Georgia. To the best of my knowledge, no Australian *premiers* attended, although many would have seen the film since. By the way, *theater* is the preferred spelling for theatrical venues in American English, but *theatre* appears in the proper name of quite a few of them, as a visit to Broadway will show.

prescribe / proscribe

Proscribing is a forbidding word and not what doctors do when they're handing out pills. They might like to *proscribe* smoking but can really only advise and leave patients to work out what's good for them.

pretentious/portentous

Portentous, *moi*? No, not if the aim is to echo Miss Piggy and her "Pretentious, *moi*?" line. To be *pretentious* is to try to look or sound cleverer or more important than is the case. A *portent* is an omen or a sign. Something that is *portentous* can be of great significance or overly solemn or pompous. Pompous, *moi*? Never.

prevaricate/procrastinate

By turning my attention to a crossword, I *procrastinated* before writing this sentence. I put off doing it. Had I been evasive about what I'd been up to, I'd have been *prevaricating*. I might not have told an outright lie but merely danced around the truth. Had I been ambiguous in trying to hide the truth, I'd have been *equivocating*. Meanwhile, does anyone have the answer for five down?

principal/principle

Principled school *principals* should be admired. It's a comment on the state of society that unprincipled 14-year-olds with spray cans at the ready and blank walls in front of them think otherwise.

prophecy/prophesy

A *prophecy* that's *prophesying* the future of humanity, or whether next Tuesday's dinner will be accompanied by mashed potato or sauerkraut, needs a *-cy* as opposed to the *-sy* for the verb.

refute/reject

Let's pretend for a moment that all is well and say *refute* means to prove something wrong as opposed to merely *rejecting* or denying it. The distinction is a useful one. Politicians who say they haven't been inserting snouts into troughs have *rejected* the allegations. Whipping out incontrovertible evidence of clean snouts and unmolested troughs would amount to *refuting*. The small-time crook who says he couldn't have burgled the factory because he was washing his hair on the night in question will have to do better than that to reach the level of *refute*.

Sensitive readers will have detected tension in the typing of the previous paragraph. Usage guide upon usage guide maintains the special place for *refute*. I intend to keep doing so – I'm attached to it and saddened by its endangerment. However, it's an irrefutable fact that the word is commonly used in the sense of a mere denial, including by journalists. I'll learn to live with this as another inevitable part of language change ... eventually. Should you care to join me as a holdout for now, we could set up a club and meet occasionally in cafes to commiserate.

reign/rein

Royals do the *reigning*, and horses are guided with *reins*. Wayward horses can be reined in; wayward royals are reduced to tabloid fodder.

sewage/sewerage

It's *sewerage* for the pipes and *sewage* for what passes through them. Misuse of these two could also go into the *sewage* category.

simple/simplistic

Simple keeps itself nice and uncomplicated. *Simplistic* comes with no hint of niceness. It means overly simplified. A simplistic solution to a problem isn't a wonderful thing as it doesn't recognise the complexities of the situation. A simplistic guide to knee surgery is not recommended reading for aspiring fixers of knee problems.

stalactite/stalagmite

Here we have a difference of two letters but an important one for people planning to live in limestone caves. The *-tites* grow down from the ceiling and the *-mites* rise up from the cave floor.

STALACVEGETITE   STALAGVEGEMITE

You could try remembering the difference by thinking that the floor-originating stalagmites *might* hurt if sat upon and the stalactites like to hold *tight* to the ceiling. Or you could Google it. That always works for me. Arguments that having so much information at our fingertips makes us dumber are so early noughties. The *-mites* and *-tites* problem is avoided should they reach out to one another to form a single pillar. They should be encouraged to do this.

stationary/stationery

A car that has had its tyres punctured will be left *stationary*; it isn't going anywhere. A cabinet filled with office supplies, although also not moving unless being wheeled somewhere, is a *stationery* cabinet in acknowledgment of the paper, pens, pencils and envelopes it contains. One way to remember the difference is to think of *paper* as ending in *-er*, which matches nicely with the *-ery* at the end of stationery. It's almost as if someone planned it that way.

tortuous/torturous

Tortuous is required for references to twisting or winding (a *tortuous* path), or lengthy and complex. *Torturous* is all about the torture meted out in forms such as electric shocks or heavy metal music piped into cells 24 hours a day. Something that's *tortuous* can also feel *torturous*. Anyone who's waded through a government report for bedtime reading can vouch for that.

uninterested/disinterested

I came upon the distinction between these two long ago, and it's a handy one at that, although I doubt there's much life left in it. While *uninterested* has the unsurprising meaning for an *un-* word of not interested, *disinterested* is associated with the notion of being without any vested interest, being impartial:

The scrupulously fair judge was disinterested throughout the extortion case. Elsewhere, the judge adjudicating on which of the divorcing parties should get custody of the family mouse mat was bored beyond measure, mind-bogglingly uninterested even.

Interestingly, these words started out about 400 years ago with their meanings around the other way. The *Merriam-Webster* dictionary people say the two then became interchangeable before the current distinction arrived. The 21st-century meaning of *uninterested* is clear. The distinction for *disinterested* is on shakier ground, particularly outside formal writing. The separate meaning isn't required often, but I find having it around is somehow reassuring, having been taught about it at an impressionable age. Should the Bill and Melinda Gates Foundation be looking for fresh causes to support, the Disinterested Protection Society could do with a cash injection of a billion or two.

us/we

Compare the pair:

We Australians eat too many jam sandwiches.
Us Australians eat too many jam sandwiches.

Leaving aside the fact one can never eat too many jam sandwiches, there's an easy way to sort one's *us* from one's *we* in sentences such as these: dispose of the noun that comes after *us* or *we* and see if a proper sentence is left.

We eat too many jam sandwiches. (proper sentence)
Us eat too many jam sandwiches. (something amiss apart from the false statement about jam sandwich consumption)

The same principle applies here:

Mum fed we kids jam sandwiches. (sorry to hear it)
Mum fed us kids jam sandwiches. (love the idea)

Remove the noun *kids* and what's left is "Mum fed we jam sandwiches" or "Mum fed us jam sandwiches". Grammatically, there's a clear winner even if the nutritional result is the same.

waive/wave

If it's *waiving* going on, a right or claim to something is being ceded. Royals reading this while standing on the balcony of Buckingham Palace in front of a crowd of tens of thousands need to drop the book and start *waving* before the republicans get wind of their distraction.

wet/whet

Why do we have a *whet* when we already have a perfectly good *wet*? Because the *whet* of *whet your appetite* has nothing to do with sogginess, no matter how mouth-watering the food before you. And a knife that's being *whetted* may undergo that procedure well away from water. If you're *whetting* a cutting implement you're sharpening it, and if you're *whetting* your appetite you're stimulating it, making it more acute.

whose/who's

Don't think of the apostrophe as indicating a possessive in *who's*. All it's doing is signalling that something has been left out, the *i* of *is* or the *ha* of *has*. It's *whose* that raises matters of possession:

Who's a pretty boy?
Whose parrot just accused me of being condescending because
I said it was a pretty boy?

Although we associate *who* and its hangers-on with people or any animal we've elevated from mere *it, whose* is used with things as well.

> *The parrot-supply company whose services I use has run out of crackers.*

your/you're

You're never going to get anyone in Hollywood to pay millions of dollars for the screen rights to *your* grammar guide. Give up now.

CHAPTER 9

THINGS TO USE AS ARGUMENT STARTERS AT PARTIES

The party's been going for hours. The few potato chips left have lost their crunch, the empty bottles are piling up and you've forgotten the names of most of the other guests. There's nothing more to be said about the weather. It's still there. It will still be there tomorrow. Sport? Too much has already been mentioned about balls being kicked, whacked with bats or clubs and sent into nets. The music sounds like a jackhammer combined with the howling of every ill-tempered dog that's ever barked and snarled in your direction. This is not a party that can get any worse. Head out to the balcony, corner that group of lawyers over by the railing and get out your grammar gripes. Go beyond grammar into other areas where language arguments dwell. The lawyers, ever lovers of a good dispute, will thank you for improving their evening.

Earlier chapters contain material to draw on – whisper *apostrophes* and watch eyes light up. Here, though, are disputes that come in a special gift box. They've been hand-picked for late-night-argument instigation. Make sure there is time left for at least half an hour of verbal duelling per topic, and be warned: they may cause hangovers.

People who use *data* as a singular deserve maximum-security jail time. Discuss.

Run *data* and *datum* together and Beethoven's Fifth Symphony comes to mind: *da-ta-da-tuuum*. A little Beethoven would be preferable to the barking-dog/jackhammer party music in the background but is of no help in deciding whether *data* is fit for use in a singular sense. The lawyers on the balcony may try to argue that because it's the plural of the Latin *datum*, it can only be a plural. On that basis, the appropriate approach would be "the *data* are" and "the *datum* is". Word on the street, though, is that *datum* doesn't get out much any more. Generalist style guides have tended to abandon it, and our inclination out on that street to use *data* in a singular sense is strong. Some academic and technical writing requires that it be a plural only, and fans of this genre feel strongly that this should remain the case. Fair enough. But in broader use, the people have spoken. By the way, there's also a reference-point-type *datum* used in measurement. This has as a plural *datums*. I don't recall the last time I encountered one of those in a newsroom. You might like to tell the lawyers about it though.

The case for not being devastated about *decimated*

Surely the misbehaving soldiers of ancient Rome faced not with a naughty mat but a punishment of having one in 10 among them killed had the most legitimate reason for getting worked up about *decimate*. The modern-day stickler has not a gory end with which to contend, but only slightly raised blood pressure at the sight of the word being used to mean something other than killing one in 10 or at least reducing by a tenth. *Decimate* gets its own special listing here because it's such a stressor for traditionalists, even though its newer meaning, to destroy a large number of or large part of, has been around for several centuries and can be widely found.

The lawyers in party mode out on the balcony may insist *decimate* comes from the Latin *decimus* for tenth and so must stick to its earlier meaning. But that was then and this is now. They might also argue it's a shame to have a precise meaning give way to a looser one. *Decimate* still keeps its Roman-soldier meaning if that's what you're after; your context will make that clear. After all, so many of our words are multitaskers, leaving us to draw on context to work out which of several meanings applies. Most of us will never need the Roman-soldier meaning. We'll also get through each day without needing a word to describe killing or destroying one in 20, one in 36 or one in 73 for that matter.

Separately, *decimation* was used for a tax of 10 per cent in England from the 17th century. In this sense, the introduction of the goods and services tax in 2000 taught consumers Australia-wide what it was like to be *decimated*.

When nouns become verbs: we can't help ourselves

Journalists are as guilty as anyone of rushing to turn nouns into verbs. For decades we've been *hospitalising* people whether they like it or not, as opposed to admitting them to hospital. If I can help it, though, no one is going to be *funeralised*. I came across the latter in copy once. The sentence asked if a certain famous actor had been *funeralised* yet. As I type this, I can report he has not, although he's closer to 100 than he is to 90. Why accept *hospital-ise* but not *funeralise*? Having been taught *hospitalise* was wrong, I used to resist and chop it out at every opportunity. But it has become an accepted part of the language. *Funeralise* has not. I'd be thrilled if *funeralise* died out never to be resurrected. It has

the odd dictionary mention and a few thousand Google results, but it has not caught on and so remains ugly and jarring, not to mention short on gravitas.

I'm confident the lawyers on the balcony wouldn't want *funeralise* as a client, but don't let them get away with suggesting turning nouns into verbs is bad all round. Nouns have been becoming verbs throughout our history of having nouns and verbs, so there's no point arguing that the process should be rejected out of hand – it's a basic part of how our language works. Any lawyer on the balcony who says otherwise needs to take a closer look at the past. There's convenience in non-verbs heading down the verb route. This can allow us to say things in shorter ways. Not that I'm recommending it, but in American English, where the noun-to-verb shift is more popular than toasted marshmallows, even *verb* has become a verb. I wouldn't be surprised to hear something like this:

Hey, did you hear that rapper dude ASAP Schlocky verbed funeral last week?

We're happy to use *contact*, *balloon*, *auction*, *model* and *host* as verbs. And who not on a low-fat or vegan diet could resist the urge to *butter* toast? Those words started out in their noun form, but verbs they also became. *Impact* is older as a verb than as a noun, although verb activity on its part still causes some people displeasure. I'm more displeased by its overuse. Psychologist, linguist and author Steven Pinker has pointed out that verbs which began as nouns or adjectives can be found in just about any paragraph of English.

Just as I hope *funeralise* doesn't take off and that none of those balcony lawyers will ever end up fighting to have it recognised in court, *elevatoring*, which I encountered recently, is another example the world doesn't need. Should you win the lawyers over to the idea that nouns becoming verbs is a natural process, stress to them the need for caution. Their formal written output should stick to tried-and-tested verbs. I still resist *to medal* and *to podium* in sport stories, but I'm resigned to defeat in the long run. No medals to be won or podium placement for me.

Adjective manipulations that have not become mainstream should be avoided too. It's a question of not going overboard by *bizarring* how we communicate. Non-bizarre fact: *bizarre* is an adjective and has not made the leap to accepted verb use. The scammers who sent a text message telling me "If you continue to overdue your credit may be affected" deserve a prison term that includes writing out 200 times a day: "We were wrong to use the adjective *overdue* as a verb and we're very, very sorry."

Dictionaries lay down the law and the law should stay put (or not)

Where did those wild-haired creatures of Scandinavian folklore go, the trolls of many a childhood? Hordes of them began to look more and more like ordinary humans, sat down at keyboards and decided that antagonising people on the internet was much more fun than lurking under bridges in fairy tales and threatening to gobble up goats. It was cold under those bridges and the goats weren't inclined to co-operate with being eaten, at least not the trio in *Three Billy Goats Gruff*. Look *troll* up in a dictionary now and internet trolling gets a prominent mention.

That's the thing about dictionaries. They provide continuity but they don't stand still. Don't let any lawyers on that balcony tell you otherwise or call for language to stay right where it is except when they come up with an invention in need of a name. Change is unsettling and not always for the better, but it is inevitable.

The increasing calls for order that came with the rise of printing led to early attempts at dictionaries. His wasn't the first, but over nine years of toil and trouble Samuel Johnson, commissioned by booksellers to help stabilise the language, rounded up 43,000 words for his highly influential list of definitions and spellings published in Britain in 1755. A more modest, and criticised, effort considered the first purely English dictionary had appeared in 1604 "for the benefit & helpe of Ladies, Gentlewomen, or any other unskilfull persons". It's nice to know someone was thinking about the ladies.

Johnson's definitions were a big improvement on previous attempts. He felt that wherever he turned there was "perplexity to be disentangled, and confusion to be regulated". His dictionary held sway until the *Oxford* came along more than a century later. And if he threw in a quirky definition or two and took the chance to settle the odd score, so be it. Party-animal lawyers should not begrudge him that. Nor should they shift the conversation to whether a class action should have been mounted to try to recoup the cost of the dictionary for readers who didn't think some definitions were giving them their money's worth.

Funds being tight and wealthy potential supporters tighter, here's how Johnson defined *patron*:

> *One who countenances, supports or protects. Commonly a wretch who supports with insolence, and is paid with flattery.*

Just to show they don't make dictionaries the way they used to, you won't find anything in a modern dictionary like Johnson's non-definition for a game popular in Elizabethan England:

> *trolmydames, noun: Of this word I know not the meaning.*

The first part of the *Oxford English Dictionary* didn't come out until 1884. Five years into the *Oxford* project, its compilers had reached the word *ant*. The word tally is now over 600,000. The lawyers on the balcony will be impressed to know that.

A changing world is bound to come up with new words and new ways of using old ones. Our major dictionaries reflect that. While we're looking to them for guidance, they're looking to see what we're getting up to with the language, and alter their entries accordingly, although let us hope the pace isn't too dizzying. Some dictionaries are more conservative and more prescriptive than others, but since the 1960s the trend has been to describe how language is used rather than preach how it should be used. That doesn't mean a free-for-all or that guidance is nowhere to be found. I like a good usage note or the word *informal* added as a method of pointing out that although the popularity of a word or a particular meaning is such that it's worthy of an entry, questions about its status remain. What I do with that information is then up to me.

As mentioned in Chapter 2, English has no language academy sending out orders. Dictionary compilers have fancy databases filled with countless real-life examples to help them decide what's going on with usage and what makes an entry appropriate. Some examples of language change will fade away; others will reach a point where resistance is futile whether everyone's finished arguing about them or not. In other cases, we forget there was ever anything being argued about.

Words run through a range of meanings over time and at the same time. The lawyers on the balcony aren't going to succeed if they try to persuade you that in calling you *silly* they're describing you as *happy* or *blessed*, as it once meant. If you're in a good mood, you could call them *nice* and make clear you're not suggesting they're *silly*, as *nice* once meant. *Naughty* once described someone who was poor, who had *naught*. It took a detour via *wicked* before ending up with the milder meaning it has today. *Egregious* went from one extreme to the other. It used to be a good thing meaning someone was distinguished, prominent in a positive way. Now anything *egregious* is remarkably bad. Vegetarians and vegans might like to look away as soon as they get to this colon: *meat* used to mean any food.

Tell those lawyers that if they come up with a new word and get enough people to use it and think of it as meaning the same thing, a dictionary entry could be their reward. If enough people then decide to give the word a different meaning, it might be added to theirs even if it's contradictory, or their meaning might be lost over time. If change goes viral, good luck trying to stop it artificially. We might lose some good meanings, but we might gain some too. That's crowdsourcing for you.

Look what they've done: the singular *they* debate

Language change can be of the subtle sort that goes on while we're not looking, or it can cause a ruckus. What's gone on with the pronoun *they* takes up an inordinate amount of space in the ruckus folder. The lawyers on the balcony are going to love sinking their teeth into this one.

They may stand there with their grammar guns blazing, insisting *they* can only be a plural, but the evidence is not with them. There are two issues here: the increasing usage in which specific people choose the *they* pronoun route for themselves ("Leslie hasn't eaten yet and they are starving"), and the one that took off in the 1960s and is to do with objections to using a generic *he* as a default to cover everyone, *he* and non-*he* alike. It might seem a recent thing, but acrimony about pronouns goes back a long way. Should you prefer your grammar sedate, this isn't the topic you're after.

Use of singular *they* and its variants to cover people in general has been around for more than 600 years. Heavyweight writers over the centuries have pulled numerous examples out of their desk drawers:

Nobody meant to be unkind, but nobody put themselves out of their way to secure her comfort.

That's Jane Austen writing in *Mansfield Park*.

Every body has their taste in noises as well as in other matters.

There she is, at it again in *Persuasion*. And did you see that space in *every body*? Shameless! Austen created singular *they* examples by the dozen. The King James Bible chipped in, and Shakespeare can easily be rumbled: Here's one of his from *Much Ado About Nothing*:

> *God send everyone their heart's desire.*

In the 18th century, grammarians huffed, puffed and cracked down on this sort of thing. Plural treatment was needed for *they* and the word wasn't to be used with singular pronouns such as *somebody*, *everybody* and *nobody*. Want to talk about a group of people in general in a sentence framed in a singular way but can't find a gender-neutral pronoun? No problem. *He*, *him* or *his* will do the job. Feminists and others would eventually have a lot to say about this ridiculous excuse for a solution, but in the meantime, I could have written the following to contented murmurings from on high:

> *A good citizen knows where he should put his pronouns.*
> *If everyone knew his pronouns, the world would be a better place.*

Critics of this approach always existed, but it was in the 1960s and 1970s that the idea of *he/him/his* having a neutral role raised widespread ire, helped along by the feminist consciousness-raising sessions 18th-century grammarians had missed out on. The idea that a person presented with a *he* would picture humans in all forms wasn't going down as well as it once did. The argument against using singular *they* persisted, even as the usage commonly snuck into people's speech while they were too busy complaining about it to notice. In formal writing, other options were pursued. We've been through phases where *he/she*, *he or she*, or *s/he* has been tried. The clunkiness rating was off the scale, and attempts to come up with anything like the following should not be made without safety goggles in place:

> *No one needs to force out of her or his brain sentences like this if she or he would rather take her or his dog for a walk.*

Some books alternated between *he* and *she* from chapter to chapter or paragraph to paragraph. Or *she* may have been used in the way *he* traditionally had been. Some people suggested being done with it and making up a new word minus the baggage of, "Is this singular and, aargh, what gender does it match?" *Ze*, *thon*, *hiser*, *heesh* and *tey* have been among the offerings, *thon* having been proposed as far back as the 1850s. Samuel Taylor Coleridge is a renowned poet, but the lawyers on the balcony would have to agree that his suggestion of replacing the generic *he* with *it* was a dud. Dennis Baron, author of the book *Grammar and Gender*, points to *ou* having been put forward in 1792 by a Scottish economist who, in a separate unhelpful suggestion, also thought what English really needed was 13 grammatical genders. Did any of the aforementioned alternatives become part of our mainstream vocabulary? Is Birdsville the capital of Australia?

In the 21st century, using *he* to represent us all is not the way to win friends. But some usage guides have maintained qualms about singular *they* despite its efficiency. I don't see a need for those qualms, but should you share them or feel formality calls for it, many a sentence can be stripped of controversy by taking a plural stance from the outset:

A well-trained lawyer knows decent arguments when he hears them. (controversial)
Well-trained lawyers know decent arguments when they hear them. (innocuous)

The increasing use of singular *they* as a pronoun by people who identify as non-binary has received the most attention in recent times. Singular *they* was named word of the year by the *Merriam-Webster Dictionary* in 2019 after online searches for it rose by more than 300 per cent compared with the previous year. The American Dialect Society, founded in 1889, named *they* its word of the decade for 2010–19. Language change can be uncomfortable. The newish usage is yet to become second nature for most of us, but it's got us talking about, in some cases yelling about, pronouns. The debate is multifaceted, but there are knock-on language effects in there somewhere. Will we end up using *they is* if talking about one person? Will *themself* become standard English? Will a different, yet to be invented pronoun take off?

Whatever the arguments, a simple "*They* has always been a plural and that's that" won't work. Let the record show that *they*, *them* and *their* have been doing singular duty for centuries and the current controversy is not the first in which they have found themselves. It's worth remembering, too, that *you* used to have *thee* and *thou* hanging around for singular purposes but bumped those out of the way to become accepted for singular and plural. We're left with "You *are* a party-animal lawyer" rather than "You *is* a party-animal lawyer" when talking to only one lawyer, but we're used to it and haven't yet felt the need to resort to a *yous are/you is* approach, at least not formally. We also have the royal *we*. Perhaps singular *they* will end up equally uncontroversial.

CHAPTER 10

THINGS THIS BOOK MIGHT BE ASKED IF IT COULD BE ASKED THINGS

What time is it?

Is noon *12pm* or *12am*? And where does midnight sit? The answer is that anyone who doesn't have a motive to create confusion should avoid the issue and stick to *noon*, *midday* and *midnight*. Do not entertain any argument that fondness for 24-hour clocks is misplaced.

Royal Museums Greenwich includes the Royal Observatory, the home in London of Greenwich Mean Time no less. Its website says most people use *12am* for midnight and *12pm* for noon. That *most* opens the door to confusion right there. In Old English, *noon* referred to about 3pm, nine hours after sunrise, but we could always pretend we didn't hear that. Further complication occurs with the knowledge that *am* stands for the Latin *ante meridiem* (before noon) and *pm* for *post meridiem* (after noon). Let's all agree it's weird to think of noon as being before or after itself outside the pages of surrealist novels. Quantum physics is also weird; maybe something could be going on there too. Oh, and midnight happens to be 12 hours before noon *and* 12 hours after noon.

The National Physical Laboratory in London describes itself as the home of UK time. It says there are no established standards for the meaning of *12am* or *12pm*. The National Institute of Standards and Technology in the US says *am* and *pm* are ambiguous in a *noon/midnight* context and shouldn't be used. The Australian government's *Style Manual* also recommends *am* and *pm* avoidance when the clock strikes 12.

The *am/pm* conundrum can even have financial consequences. A commenter years ago in a thread on the *Guardian* website complained he had been asked by his bank to pay in money by *12pm* on a particular day to avoid charges. Not sharing the bank's view that *12pm* was midday, he handed over the funds at 3.07pm. A phone call was required to get the charges waived. Neither party budged on what constituted proper use of *12pm*.

Will my head literally explode as I read this?

Not long after they learn to walk, tiny future subeditors are taught that if something is *literally* so, it really is so. If it *literally* happens, it really happens. Did your head just *literally* explode. No? Still intact and where it's always been? Thought so. Did you *literally* hit the roof when you saw how many toast crumbs were holding a party down the back of your sofa? Only figuratively, you say sheepishly. Well and good.

Meanwhile, a breakaway group of tiny non-subeditors throughout the land decided from their earliest days that *literally* works fine as an all-purpose way of adding emphasis, just as *absolutely* or *totally* do. No *literally* of mine or that comes my way for subediting will be allowed to be used figuratively. I like the distinction and feel there's life left in it yet. Not literal life, but, oh, you know what I mean.

I think of my tuba-playing talents as very unique. Is that OK?

I would never be one to judge tuba skills. I'm just not judgmental in that way. Don't know why. Never have been. To place a *very* next to *unique*, however, is something I must caution against. Just as tiny future subeditors are taught about *literally*, they are taught that no *unique* worthy of its uniqueness should associate with a *very*, a *mostly*, a *little bit* or any of their co-conspirators. In its pure form, *unique* is the only one of its kind. Something or someone is either *unique* or not. If your tuba skills are *unique* there's nothing else like them. *A little bit unique* or *a lot unique* is to logic what a golf ball is to chess: unhelpful. As we've seen, however, meanings drift, and since the 19th century a weaker, controversial meaning of unusual or remarkable crept into *unique* when no one was paying attention, as is so often the way. I'm sticking to the prime meaning and suggest you're more likely to impress if you do too. Allowance may be made for *almost unique*. The second-last remaining exclamatory paradise whydah (it's a bird with a ridiculously long tail and it thanks you for asking) has the right to call itself *almost unique* as it awaits the day true uniqueness arrives.

Someone described a chocolate bar as awesome the other day. I thought it was just so-so. Am I missing something?

I'm glad you asked. You may be trying to cling on to *awesome*'s early meaning, the one about inspiring great awe, huge respect mingled with wonder or fear. However, the word has suffered quite a comedown in everyday speech. These days chocolate bars, gym workouts, chewing gum and paying for a packet of tissues are all at risk of being described as *awesome*. It's become an overused way of saying something is pretty good, cool, even just mildly pleasing. We could think of that as awfully annoying, but we wouldn't be sticking to the original meaning of *awful* if we did; inspiring dread and/or wonder isn't what *awful* gets up to much any more either. It came upon its reduced circumstances earlier than *awesome*, so we're more used to the change, not that I'll ever stop thinking of *awesome* overuse as dreadful. By *dreadful* I mean really bad and unpleasant as opposed to that word's older meaning to do with great fear. Is it just me or is there a pattern emerging here?

I want to use *centred around*. Who's going to stop me?

I will if I get the opportunity and you're not bigger than I am. I used it once in secondary school, had my teacher point out the lack of logic, one thing being around and the other being central and all that, and have been a *centred on/revolved around* person ever since. *Centred around* is commonly used, but you'll look so much more careful if you avoid it.

Can I carry on irregardless?

Step away from *irregardless*. It appears in dictionaries but along with hints that it's iffy. *Irregardless* is a blend of *regardless* and *irrespective* best kept out of written English. Throw it into the odd social media post if you must, but only when you have few followers and aren't at risk of going viral and influencing wider society. The *-less* on the end of *regardless* tells us there's no regarding going on. An *ir-* at the start signals the same thing. A signal at one end will do, and I don't mean making it *irregard*. Consider *irregardless* as being a waste of a perfectly good *ir-* that could be doing proper work at the start of *irrespective*.

Do journalists ever feel physically imperilled if they miss a deadline?

No, but it would be understandable if we did. Douglas Adams, he of *The Hitchhiker's Guide to the Galaxy*, joked about being a fan of the whoosh they made as they went right on by. Whooshes sound benign, but there's a reason there's a *dead* in *deadline*. In the American Civil War, it was a line around a prison. Guards had guns, they knew how to use them, and prisoners trying to cross deadlines risked a fate worse than making editors angry.

Can I call my novelty barbecue tongs iconic? They're well known in the neighbourhood.

Stopping *iconic* on its march towards global domination is a noble aim, but hope has long left the building, probably to scurry after an iconic Elvis. It's become the go-to word for anything or anyone remotely famous and representative of something or well regarded. It's not the shift in meaning from religious imagery that's the problem, but the numbing overuse that knows no bounds.

Journalists are particularly guilty. A cursory database search covering newspapers of all stripes around Australia brought up dozens of examples pumped out over the course of just a few days. This nation has iconic cabins, parkas, moments, songs and bathing boxes. You can pop into an iconic cafe, watch an iconic soap opera, get tourist information at an iconic visitor centre, look up at an iconic lighthouse, curse an iconic swooping magpie or buy tooth-rotting items at an iconic lolly shop. Milk, you might like to know, is an "iconic dairy term". I once came across a reference to iconic stains of the penguin poo variety. Bear in mind, too, that it's often best to say nothing. No one needs to be told that the Sydney Opera House is famous or iconic. Even Melburnians know that.

What's this about verbs starting with capital letters?

Some of us choose to *Google* and some to *google*. Capital *P Photoshopping* and *photoshopping* are being undertaken somewhere in the world right now. To *Facebook* or *facebook*, that is the question. Dictionaries give both options in these cases, but I reach for the capitals as a nod to their status as brands. A company that has its name or that of its product turned into a verb may be thrilled by its popularity or vexed by the downside of the name becoming so generic no one remembers that there's a company out there in the first place. The man who became Uber's chief executive in 2017, Dara Khosrowshahi, considered it cool to be at the head of a company with verb written all over it. We'll put him in the glass half-full category. The issue is one for the marketers and trademark lawyers to argue about while the world goes on its merry verb-making way. We've Googled our way to the point of no return. Companies have a noun issue too as their brands become associated with a type of product in general. The Frisbee, Kleenex and Doona people know all about that. Those names remain trademarks but *escalator* and *yo-yo* lost the fight.

I was tagging a wall the other day and someone said I'd created a magnificent piece of graffito. Were they right?

They were right and wrong. *Graffito* is the singular form of *graffiti*, so the over-praiser who complimented you was correct about that. However, hardly any English-speakers use the word *graffito*, so it might as well not exist as far as we're concerned. As it can be confidently said that your tagging was in no way magnificent, it would be best if no more of that existed either.

Should I fuss about *only*?

This takes us back to the misbehaving modifiers chastised in Chapter 6. There are two ways to treat *only*. One is to be unwaveringly strict about putting it next to the word it's talking about, driving away any ambiguity monster that may be salivating at the thought of rampaging through the sentence at hand. Here's how *only* can bounce about and change a sentence's meaning:

Only Taylor dreamt of becoming a tiger pedicurist. (Wisely, no one else wanted the job.)

Taylor dreamt only of becoming a tiger pedicurist. (She dreamt of nothing else, suggesting a lack of imagination.)

Taylor dreamt of becoming only a tiger pedicurist. (She didn't want to be a tiger teeth cleaner as well or a tiger whisker groomer.)

Taylor dreamt of becoming the only tiger pedicurist. (She wanted the job all to herself.)

Taylor dreamt of becoming a pedicurist to anaesthetised tigers only. (She wasn't interested in the awake and snarling ones.)

I like to keep an eye on what my *only*s are up to, but I also accept the view that being too strict about where they go can lead to an unnatural result. Context has a key role in banishing the ambiguity monster. It's the natural way of things that we like to put our *only*s between the subject and the verb:

I only wore four dresses on my wedding day, but I had a fifth one on standby.

A stickler would say the *only* in that example needs to come after *wore* to ensure the intended meaning that four out of five dresses were worn. But it's impossible to imagine anyone taking the point of that sentence as being that the dresses were only worn, that the bride didn't do anything else to them: spill wine on them maybe, rip the hems while floundering on the dance floor, or hoist the dresses high to display her latest thigh tattoo.

In the song title *I Only Have Eyes for You*, what we have is *I* being a fine subject and *have* a fine verb. The *only* between them is doing what comes naturally and creating a pleasing rhythm. The song's been around since the 1930s. Only people spending too long in the company of 18th-century grammar books are likely to insist that a listener could take it to mean the singer has not a heart, a hand, a foot or a Swiss bank account to spare for the beloved of choice, but only a couple of beady eyes.

In the next sentence, ambiguity does arise:

I warned the bridesmaids only about staying away from the annoying wannabe tiger pedicurist my mum made me invite.

Were the bridesmaids the only ones warned or were they warned only about the tiger pedicurist and no one else? The way the words are stressed in speech would make the meaning clear. In writing, extra discipline helps. If the meaning is that the bridesmaids were the only ones cautioned, place the *only* after warned, or at least between *I* and *warned*.

Whatever I do with *however* is right, isn't it?

If what you're doing is any of the following, we are as one:

However I use however, *I respect it.*
However, not everyone is as careful.

I know, however, we're all capable of change when threatened with medieval torture methods.

In the first example, the initial *however* is standing in for *no matter how*. In the second and third, it's doing *nevertheless* duty and comes with a comma. If it's the following anyone is up to, and I have seen a disturbing number of people get up to it, all is not well:

I promise to change, however I won't do it just yet.

In that case *however* is being used as a simple substitute for *but*, which isn't the done thing. It has greater ambitions than that. If you don't want to throw in a *but*, consider one of these:

I promise to change; however, I won't do it just yet.
I promise to change. However, I'll probably need to be tortured before I get around to it.

Why hasn't someone cleaned up the spelling mess?

There's no pleasing some people. Just because *rough*, *plough*, *though*, *cough* and *through* are all pronounced differently, they think something needs to be done about spelling. Faced with a *scourge*, they *urge* action. In fact, most of our words are orderly enough, but the offending examples are so common they vex learners born into an English-speaking environment or trying to tame the beast as a second or third language. Even if we reach a stage where nothing is written by hand and keyboards are obsolete because speech-to-text software is perfect or our devices turn our thoughts into text (aka the end of civilisation as we know it), studies show the importance of good spelling to reading ability. Suffice to say, our spelling system has plenty of vexing to do yet.

Reasons for our spelling mess were mentioned in Chapter 1. Settling on an alphabet with too few letters to cover all our sounds was regrettable. Combine that with factors such as pilfering on a grand scale from other languages, a mistake or 20, changes in pronunciation, and the way the printing press took off. It's a tangled web we weave even when not trying to deceive.

Noah Webster with his *-er* and *-or* endings left his mark on American spelling, even if not all his changes were adopted. Other prominent individuals and spelling-reform associations have not fared as well. Even an American president tried, and that's not a reference to Donald Trump's freewheeling social media habits. In 1906 Theodore Roosevelt ordered the US Government Printing Office to adopt 300 simplified spellings. Hearts and minds were not with him, and he soon backtracked. Starting in 1934, the *Chicago Daily Tribune* went on a crusade for "sane" spelling, not giving up on the remnants of its unsuccessful campaign until 1975. Dozens of unorthodox spellings appeared in its articles over the years, including *bazar, burocrat, clew, hocky, fantom, hammoc, iland, yern* and *thoro.*

In Australia, a public servant and spelling reformer named Harry Lindgren pushed from the 1960s for a gradual approach to change, starting with *e* as in *bet*. *Friend* would be *frend* and *death* would be *deth*. But they wouldn't be – his ideas didn't take off. The English Spelling Society, based in the UK, has been pushing for simplification since 1908. On it pushes.

A major obstacle to change is our attachment to tradition. Most of us come to an accommodation with the way things are. We learn to spell thousands of words, and it's the unfamiliar reform suggestions that look odd. But the problem is thornier than that. If we tried for a simplified, global spelling system, how would we agree on which spellings to adopt? There is no universal accent for people who speak the diverse range of *Englishes* out there. Whose pronunciation would prevail in a more phonetic system? And what, my frend, would we do about the mountain of writing in the old spellings? No wonder people feel the need to giv up. Or maybe there's sumthing to be sed for a gradual aproach.

Yes, but how do I sort out my -ables from my -ibles?

Lacking optimism about spelling reform, are you? Should independence from modern technology be your thing, you could take a retro position and try *-able/-ible* memorisation mantras, or you could try learning Latin, although that will only get you so far. Lists of rules exist but exceptions will trip you up. Looking on the bright side, there are hundreds more *-able* words than *-ible* words, so guessing the former comes with a higher chance of success. New *-able* words keep appearing but the *-ibles* are blasts from the past. The situation may appear *incomprehensible*, but the truth is it's *manageable*.

LAST THINGS LAST

A trip in a time machine to 200 years into the future to see what English is getting up to would be intriguing. Change is a certainty. Looking at the big picture, will the language's myriad versions around the world have drifted further apart? Will it retain its global status as a lingua franca? Will technology and power shifts lead to more uniformity? Would someone from today be bamboozled? Will the startling advances we're already seeing in the ability of artificial intelligence to create text that looks like a human wrote it mean no humans ever write anything beyond shopping lists? Looking at the minuscule picture, will *iconic* still be overused? Will the apostrophe make it through? Will *thou* and *thee* stage a shock comeback and become regular reality show contestants? Will the past tense of the verb *to read* finally get the *red* spelling it deserves?

I'd want my money back if I took a package tour to the 23rd century only to land in the middle of an argument over a split infinitive. Should the landscape be a wasteland and society dystopian, a 10 per cent refund would do, but full reimbursement for split infinitive disputation would be the only reasonable response.

Back here in the present, texting and social media have meant that so much is published by so many every second of every day with no sign of a filter. The informality, LOLs, trolls and rapid pace that the online world enables have made much writing more akin to the most unbridled examples of talking. This can be viewed as evidence of different levels of formality being used in different settings. Or, for the more fearful, it's yet another sign that language Armageddon is nigh. A decent proportion of "manglers of/creative experimenters with" English have a reasonable idea of what's appropriate where and when, and know how to write with greater formality and care when the setting calls for it. We shouldn't judge the language's health by the most inarticulate examples we find.

English is robust. Social media and text-speak have been changing it, OMG, as people play around with ways to get a message across, but change is nothing it hasn't seen before and won't see again. That's not to say there isn't plenty of egregious and toxic content on social media, but that's a topic for another book. Isn't it always the way? The bigger the crowd you let into the party, the messier things get and the more likely it is that someone will be intent on trashing the joint.

I'm not in the camp that fears it's all downhill for English from here. We've plenty of successful communicating to do yet, and even emojis are part of that. I'd squirm, at least for a decade or so, should smiley faces and their friends start cropping up everywhere in standard journalism, editorialising on the subject at hand, but I'm happy to use them elsewhere. I can reveal that behind the scenes at my workplace we've created our own little messaging system using symbols such as dancing penguins, sunglasses-wearing smileys and eagles. No more will be revealed about those. To provide a glossary would be to give away trade secrets. Suffice to say we like our dancing penguins, they work hard for us, they speed up communication, we feed them well and we keep them in their place. They're an addition to our words in the right context rather than a threat to them.

Dear English, you're not perfect and never will be. We grumble and argue about you, but that doesn't mean we're not fond of you. Grammar and usage basics matter, but they're not your whole story. You're untidy. You're dynamic. You're exuberant. You're expressive. Deployed well, you've given us great literature, great clarity of thought, great elegance, great ways of saying what needs to be said. Keep up the good work.

ACKNOWLEDGMENTS

I can't help but think music is going to start up in my head as I write this. The publishing industry must have an equivalent of the unsubtle "wrap it up or be dragged off stage" orchestral hint people doing a lot of thanking at American award shows face. However, there is gratitude to be expressed and I'm going to set myself the challenge of expressing it before any conductors employed by publishers to rein in acknowledgment sections raise their batons.

This book grew out of two things on which I've worked. One is the style guide used by *The Age*, *The Sydney Morning Herald*, *The Australian Financial Review*, the *Brisbane Times* and *WAtoday*. For the past few years, I've also written a weekly in-house word-wrestling column that takes itself less seriously than the style guide. Its readers have sent me off on a wide range of research expeditions in search of answers to thorny language questions. Newsrooms are full of people who love asking thorny questions, which is just as well when you think about it.

So it's thanks to all the style-guide compilers and contributors past and present, and to the *Tuesday Tips* correspondents with their thorny questions. Thanks also to Mark Fuller, who suggested doing something like *Tuesday Tips* in the first place; to Gay Alcorn for being so supportive of the idea of a book; and to Angus Holland, Felicity Lewis, Alex Kaplan, Michael Schlechta and Wade Pearce for invaluable sounding-board provision and advice during the "How is this doable?" phase. Thanks to Matt Golding for his zeal in providing such wonderful cartoons, and to the rest of the team I work with at *The Age* and our sister publications.

I'm grateful also to Jane Willson of Murdoch Books for asking me to write this book and for her enthusiasm, support and guidance. Thanks to everyone else at Murdoch Books who has been involved, particularly editor Nicola Young, who provided countless wise suggestions and corrections.

The T-word (note the capital T) goes out to all my friends. I'll take this opportunity to single out Jacinta Reddan, unofficial publicist and early insister there was a book to be written; Rosanne Michie, talker-through of all manner of things bookish and provider of the Don Quixotian sailboard riders so crucial to my subediting career; Teresa Murphy, patient listener during long book chats; and Chris Hornsey, sharer of words of book wisdom.

Last but the opposite of least, a big thanks to my family – Gary and Tessie – for putting up with me, not that I give them much choice.

BIBLIOGRAPHY

Bragg, Melvyn *The Adventure of English: The Definitive Biography of Our Language* (Sceptre, 2016)

Bryson, Bill *Bryson's Dictionary of Troublesome Words: A Writer's Guide to Getting it Right* (Broadway Books, 2002)

Bryson, Bill *Mother Tongue* (Penguin Books, 2008)

Butterfield, Jeremy (editor) *Fowler's Concise Dictionary of Modern English Usage* (Third Edition, Oxford University Press, 2016)

Crystal, David *The Fight for English: How Language Pundits Ate, Shot and Left* (Oxford University Press, 2006)

Crystal, David *Spell It Out: The Curious, Enthralling and Extraordinary Story of English Spelling* (Picador, 2014)

Crystal, David *Making a Point: The Persnickety Story of English Punctuation* (St Martin's Press, 2015)

Dreyer, Benjamin *Dreyer's English: An Utterly Correct Guide to Clarity and Style* (Arrow Books, 2020)

Duffy, Claire *The Australian Students' Guide to Writing and Grammar* (NewSouth Publishing, 2019)

Griffin, Simon *F—ing Apostrophes: A Guide to Show You Where You Can Stick Them* (Icon Books, 2016)

Hudson, Nicholas *Oxford Modern Australian Usage* (Oxford University Press Australia, 1997)

Kamm, Oliver *Accidence Will Happen: A Recovering Pedant's Guide to English Language and Style* (Pegasus Books, 2016)

McWhorter, John *The Power of Babel: A Natural History of Language* (Times Books, Henry Holt and Company, 2001)

Marsh, David *For Who the Bell Tolls: The Essential and Entertaining Guide to Grammar* (Guardian Books and Faber & Faber 2014)

Murray-Smith, Stephen *Right Words: A Guide to English Usage in Australia* (Viking, 1989)

Norris, Mary *Between You & Me: Confessions of a Comma Queen* (W.W. Norton, 2016)

Pinker, Stephen, *The Sense of Style: The Thinking Person's Guide to Writing in the 21st Century* (Penguin Books, 2015)

Taggart, Caroline *Misadventures in the English Language* (Michael O'Mara Books, 2016)

Truss, Lynne *Eats, Shoots & Leaves* (Gotham Books, 2006)

Zinsser, William, *On Writing Well: The Classic Guide to Writing Nonfiction* (Harper Perennial, 2016)

So many hundreds of thousands of words out there; so little time to look them all up. In the preparation of this book, the following online dictionaries have provided information, inspiration and entertainment via numerous articles and blog posts, as well as definition-delving resources: the Google English dictionary, provided by Oxford Languages (part of Oxford University Press); oed.com; collinsdictionary.com; merriam-webster.com; macquariedictionary.com.au; dictionary.cambridge.org; and the Online Etymology Dictionary (etymonline.com).

INDEX

Index

Index